GOD
GLASSES

Changing Your Vision for Life

by Linda M. Young

ISBN: 978-0-9841617-0-6
Published by Ray and Linda Young
Palm Desert, CA

Printed in the United States of America

30% Total recycled fiber

We will preserve more natural environments for future generations with recycled products. We are making every effort to move toward 100% recycled resources in our products. ~ Please recycle :)

Contents

My love and thanks to God, who is able to do exceedingly abundantly above all that I could ever ask or think. Your unconditional love has flooded my life.

To my wonderful husband and best friend, Ray. You have supported me in everything I have ever wanted to accomplish. My favorite part of life has been hanging out with you.

My sincere thanks to my family, friends and dedicated ministry team. Together, we are taking this message to the nations.

Linda

Foreword

God Glasses by author, Linda Young, is a solid theological treatise that is both fun to read and practical in its application, no matter where you are on your spiritual journey. The love of God unfolds in every chapter and is underscored each step of the way. As I read the manuscript, I cried at times as I was moved by the glorious revelation this book emphasizes.

To be clear, *God Glasses* is not about positive thinking or controlling the universe through the power of your mind. It is not about self-esteem either. Instead, Linda shows us how the facts we see don't necessarily equate to truth. She reminds us that God sees differently than we do and tells us how God Glasses can correct our vision—not by denying the truth—by revealing it! Linda wants us to know we can start seeing more than our natural eyes are capable of showing us when we understand how we can get our own pair of God Glasses.

In the very first chapter of *God Glasses*, Linda tackles salvation theology and makes it the basis for seeing life clearly.

Restoring our friendship with God is essential to lasting life change that puts a new and amazing spin on the way we see life.

The powerful truths of this book touched me deeply, as they will you. Whether you need to see God or the members of your own family differently, *God Glasses* will allow you to see them from a perspective of truth. If you are struggling with temporal things like poor health, lack of provision, or an anemic prayer life, this book will show you how to see these problems clearly, from God's perspective.

Linda does a fabulous job of fostering a desire to get to know God and understand His nature so you can develop your personal relationship with Him. She has certainly maintained her biblical integrity in this book, while making it practical for everyone.

God Glasses challenged me to change my way of thinking in order to see life from God's perspective. Solomon wrote, *"As he thinks in his heart, so is he."* (Proverbs 23:7) Changed thinking and a fresh perspective are what we all need to move forward. *God Glasses* not only points us to God's written guide for how life is to be lived, but also encourages us to develop a personal, one-on-one relationship with Him.

Linda asked me for my theological analysis of this book— *I confirm it*! Now my personal feelings—*I love it*!

God Glasses is a great read. My prayer is that God will send this book around the world.

Mike Harrison, M. Div., D. Min.
Pastor, Church 212°
Palm Desert, CA
www.church212.com

Hello Lord,

I'm coming to You today because I want to know You more. I want to see You better. I want to draw closer to all the things You have for me. I want to see my life the way You do.

As I read this book and learn more about You, please open my eyes so I can see You more clearly. Help me to receive everything You have made available to me through Your Word. I pray these things in the Name of Your one and only Son, Jesus.

Love,
Me

Introduction

Several years ago, while getting dressed for an appointment, something strange happened to me. The day had appeared like most. Normal. Routine. I certainly wasn't expecting a life-changing, path-defining journey to be launched the moment I attempted to pin my favorite rhinestone accessory to my jacket.

"Wait a minute. Surely this cannot be happening. Not to *me*," was my whispered denial. I didn't know which was worse: not being able to focus my eyes on a clasp that had *obviously* shrunk overnight or the never-gonna-happen-to-me, over-the-age-of-forty thing that happens to our eyes.

Being of the Boomer Generation, I was a card-carrying, self-proclaimed member of the Age-Defying Denial Club. Aging process? What? Me? Never! That happens to older people! It's not a part of my DNA! But whoa, the truth is the truth. Try as I might, I couldn't focus on that tiny clasp. I squinted hard, straining to focus but my vision was just too blurred. "I can do this," I thought as I willed my eyes to see, "Surely if I just try harder..."

Later that afternoon, newly purchased drugstore reading glasses in hand, I picked up my rhinestone pin again to give it another try. Would I really be able to see this time? In a second, the clasp clicked into place with ease. The problem was never a mysteriously shrinking metal clasp. The problem was my ability to see correctly. I needed glasses if I was going to have my perfect 20/20 vision restored.

To be clear, my eye-opening journey has nothing to do with fashion jewelry. It is a journey about seeing life correctly, from God's perspective. We may have one view when we look at our family, health, finances, or future, but many times our view of life is not in sync with God's. Did you even know He has a view? He sees perfectly! He clearly and accurately sees the perfect plan for your life, all the way down to the last detail. Jeremiah 29:11 says:

"For I know the plans I have for you,' declares the Lord, 'plans to prosper you and not to harm you, plans to give you hope and a future.'"

God wants us to see things from His perspective, so we need His kind of glasses. I like to call them "God Glasses." Of course, God Glasses can't be bought at a store; the brick and mortar kind or the online kind. But you can have them, and the best news is they're free.

I invite you to come with me now and learn about your own God Glasses. Once you learn what they are, you will never want to take them off. They have the ability to change you, your circumstances, and the way you live the rest of your life. You're going to love wearing them. They will give you beauty from the inside out.

So come on! Turn the page. Perfect 20/20 is vision just ahead!

TO CLING
TO GOD
AND TO THE
THINGS OF
GOD—THIS
MUST BE
OUR MAJOR
EFFORT, THIS
MUST BE
THE ROAD
THE HEART
FOLLOWS.

–JOHN CASSIAN

one

the truth about
WHAT WE SEE

Have you ever read the message on the outside mirror of your car? It warns, "Objects in mirror are closer than they appear." So, although you see an object in that mirror, it's telling you your view is distorted and incorrect—in other words, what you think you see is not the truth.

In the same way, it is possible your assessments of life, circumstances, and people may not be the truth. There are facts and then there is truth, but they are not necessarily the same. Throughout this book, we will look at examples of how these two perspectives can differ significantly. You see, God has a different way of seeing things than we do. While He doesn't deny the facts, He does view them through the truth and power of His Word. He wants us to be able to see as clearly as He does. He wants us to put on our God Glasses. That's great news!

"Yes, that *is* great news! ...Wait a minute. What are God Glasses anyway?" you ask.

Simply put, God Glasses are God's point of view on everything. God Glasses provide you with proper light, clear vision, and a bright future. God Glasses change your assessment of a situation by changing your heart through His perspective and His truth. Once you start wearing them, you will begin to see people and situations through God's viewpoint, and not your own. God Glasses correct how you see things and increase your ability to see what God sees that your natural eyes cannot. When you make a decision to lay down your previous beliefs and traditional responses that have been based on your natural senses, God Glasses will not only change your perception, they will change your circumstances, and ultimately, they will change your life. The benefits of God Glasses are amazing. They allow you to have 20/20 vision from God's standpoint.

"So, how do I get myself a pair of these fabulous glasses?" I knew you were going to ask.

You can see the way God does by pursuing a personal friendship with Him. Get to know Him. Learn about who He is. Find out what He likes and what He doesn't like. Talk to Him. Read about Him. Study His nature and character. Spend time with Him. The more you understand Him, the more you will be able to see clearly from His point of view. You can learn a great deal about Him in His Word and by spending time with Him in prayer and conversation. Just hang out with Him!

Once you have His vision, your filters will become vibrantly alert and alive to the value of people and the possibilities of success in all areas of your life. No matter what the situation, God's perspective is always the truth. Seeing as He sees will be liberating, even in how you perceive God. John 8:32 teaches us, *"Then you will know the truth, and the truth will set you free."*

Did you really read that verse? It says, "Then you will know the truth…" In other words, it is the Truth you *know* that sets you free!

"And how much is this going to cost?" Oh, you're going to love this. You see, God Glasses are not only priceless, they are free.

One interesting, simple, yet complex and mysterious characteristic of God is that He will not force His will on you. When He created you, He gave you the gift of free will. That remarkable gift gives you the right to choose for yourself what you will believe and live by, and what you will ignore and avoid. Daily life is filled with constant choices and your choices have consequences that will deliver good or bad results. You can make wise choices if you are wearing your God Glasses.

Have you ever had the kind of day that makes you wish you had just stayed in bed with the covers over your head? The alarm goes off and everything seems to go wrong—and you didn't even hit the snooze button! You walk sleepy-eyed into the kitchen to find coffee all over the counter and realize that last night you slipped the coffee pot into the brewer crooked; you attempt to turn your computer on and stare, unbelieving, at a lifeless black screen—your computer has crashed for no apparent reason; then your nose tells you the dog didn't quite make it outside and he thought the new hallway carpeting was good enough for the task at hand. Bad day? Well, in the natural, yes, the day has begun poorly, but when you put on your God Glasses, your day can turn around for the good. How? By looking at it from God's perspective and choosing to agree with God rather than your circumstances.

This is the day the Lord has made—you can rejoice and be glad in it! You can do *all* things through Him who strengthens you! (See Psalm 118:24 and Philippians 4:13.) Sometimes we just need to see the joy, or perhaps I should say the humor, when things seem to go wrong.

God has such great love for you! He wants to help you through each day and He will equip you to get through every adverse situation, no matter how bad it is.

God has provided His Word to help us navigate through life. We use our God Glasses to understand Scripture and see everything around us as God would see. When we have God's perspective, we respond to life and people differently. Unconditional love and acceptance begins to pour out of us and impossible situations suddenly become a piece of cake.

Perhaps now would be a good time to look back to the beginning, when God created Adam and Eve. *"Then God said, "Let Us make man in Our image, in Our likeness, and let them rule over the fish of the sea and the birds of the air, over the livestock, over all the earth, and over all the creatures that move along the ground."* (Genesis 1:26) When God said, "Let Us make man in Our image" and "in Our likeness," He didn't mean we would have His eye color or be as tall as Him. He was saying we were to have God's authority here on earth. God created us so He could have a friendship with us!

God loved Adam and Eve and withheld nothing from them. His only command was not to eat of a certain tree. *"The Lord God took the man and put him in the Garden of Eden to work it and take care of it. And the Lord God commanded the man, "You are free to eat from any tree in the garden; but you must not eat from the tree of the knowledge of good and evil, for when you eat of it you will surely die."* (Genesis 2:15-17) As long as they obeyed God and didn't eat of that tree, their life was wonderful. They enjoyed fellowship with God. In a sense, they lived life wearing God Glasses, seeing everything correctly with perfect vision through God's perfect perspective and perfect truth. They operated in the authority God gave them in the Garden and lived an abundantly healthy, vibrant life. And God said, "It was good."

Then everything changed. Satan arrived on the scene with lies and temptations, much the same as he does in our lives today. He whispered the blasphemous, disgusting lie that God was holding back from Adam and Eve. Tragically they took the bait. They chose to believe the father of lies over the Father of Truth and when they did, it was as though their God Glasses—that which had allowed them to see as God sees—slipped from their eyes and fell to the ground, shattered beyond human ability to repair.

Adam and Eve became vision impaired the moment they bought into Satan's lie and could no longer discern the truth. Darkness entered their lives. No longer were they able to experience life as God intended. Romans 1:20-21 explains to us exactly what happened: *"For since the creation of the world God's invisible qualities—His eternal power and divine nature—have been clearly seen, being understood from what has been made, so that men are without excuse. For although they knew God, they neither glorified Him as God nor gave thanks to Him, but their thinking became futile and their foolish hearts were darkened."*

Although Adam and Eve disobeyed God's one and only command to them, His love for them and all of mankind remained great. While they were incapable of doing anything to fix their relationship with Him, God had a plan already in place. Before the foundation of the earth, His master plan was for Jesus to become the bridge between us so that we could have the opportunity to enjoy the rightful, wonderful relationship Adam and Eve had once shared with Him in the Garden.

All the necessary steps for restoration had already been taken by God. The entire New Testament is a story of how God renewed our relationship with Him through Jesus. *"For God so loved the world that He gave His one and only Son, that whoever believes in Him shall not perish but have eternal life."* (John 3:16)

Without God Glasses, we are all vision impaired. Each one of us has tremendous need of the precious gift only Jesus can give because of the remarkable price He paid for us. *"We all, like sheep, have gone astray, each of us has turned to his own way; and the Lord has laid on Him the iniquity of us all."* (Isaiah 53:6) Jesus is the *Answer.* Jesus is the *Way* and He is the *Truth.* The sins of the entire world were stamped "Paid in Full" when He became the atoning sacrifice, as proclaimed in 1 John 2:2. He is the only One to pay our ransom, the only One able to offer us restored relationship with God. The Bible actually tells us that Jesus, who knew no sin, became sin for us so we could become the righteousness of God. God loves us so much. He offers us the chance to restore our friendship with Him through Jesus and a chance to get our own personal pair of God Glasses.

Even though the price was paid, is paid, and will forever remain paid, we still have to choose to believe Jesus is who He and God's Word say He is. God will never force the truth of His Word down our throats. He simply holds it out to us as the most precious gift containing the ability to radically change our lives, restore us, and make us whole again. There is a catch, however. We can't pay for it. We can only freely receive it.

When we freely receive what God wants to give to us and we accept all He has done for us, it is our way of telling Him, "Yes, God, I want to be part of Your kingdom." We put on our God Glasses by choosing Him.

Life is jam-packed with challenging personal relationships and human interactions. It is no small feat trying to handle them all the right way! We have our natural families, blended families, in-laws, out-laws, employers, employees, co-workers, customers, neighbors, friends, and unfortunately sometimes we even have enemies. *Whew!* How do we manage all these complicated relationships without exploding?

How do we deal with the co-worker with the half-gallon-sized coffee mug who drains the last drop of coffee from our freshly made pot, but never makes more for the next person? Or, what do we do when we attempt to make a first-time call to a store we want to do business with, only to have their computerized telephone tree ask us to spell the last name of a person we've neither met, nor heard of? That interaction alone can drive a perfectly sane person to rage within seconds! Worse yet, what about the sales clerk who can only shift into one gear?—park.

Where, oh where, are our God Glasses when we need them???

It seems that sometimes the minefield of life is littered with explosives with your name on them, just waiting to take you out. Put on your God Glasses and you will be able to see clearly and avoid those bombs more often than not.

When I have my God Glasses on, I can see things I wouldn't otherwise see because my own impaired sight would cater to my natural whims and fleshly inclinations. If I'm making choices and reacting based on how I feel rather than the better way God has for me, I'm operating in my own wisdom. God provides us with His wisdom when we are willing to put on our God Glasses. This wisdom is not available anywhere else and yet, it's free.

First Corinthians 2:6-10 (MSG) helps explain God's perspective on wisdom. "*We, of course, have plenty of wisdom to pass on to you once you get your feet on firm spiritual ground, but it's not popular wisdom, the fashionable wisdom of high-priced experts that will be out-of-date in a year or so. God's wisdom is something mysterious that goes deep into the interior of His purposes. You don't find it lying around on the surface. It's not the latest message, but more like the oldest—what God determined as the way to bring out His best in us, long before we ever arrived on the scene. The experts of our day haven't a clue about what this eternal plan is. If they had, they wouldn't have killed the Master of the God-designed life on a cross. That's why we have this Scripture text: 'No one's ever seen or heard anything like this, never so much as imagined anything quite like it—what God has arranged for those who love Him.' But you've seen and heard it because God by His Spirit has brought it all out into the open before you.*"

True wisdom comes from spending time with our God Glasses on while we study God's Word, understanding who God is, and asking Him to let us see from His perspective. It is our choice. We might notice people around us, even at church, who we expect to behave the way God would want them to, yet they don't. You may wonder, "How can this be?" This is because wearing God

Glasses is a choice, a purposeful decision to see and behave God's way. It's not something that automatically happens when you join a church. As you choose to listen and obey His voice, you are in essence putting on your God Glasses. Understanding who He is, His revelation to us, and the things He desires for our lives comes by walking in the wisdom He provides.

God's wisdom is found in His Word, which is the Bible, and through His Spirit, who He sends to live inside of you once you receive His Son, Jesus. God has so much He wants to reveal to your heart. He will reveal it as you spend time with Him.

Wearing God Glasses is a choice, just like wearing regular glasses is. Sometimes we put them on and sometimes we take them off because they might feel uncomfortable. We can allow an I-don't-feel-like-putting-forth-the-extra-effort-to-seek-God mindset to seep into our lives. Before we know it, we are right back into depending on our own wisdom instead of God's and wondering why our relationship with Him is not as strong as it used to be, having drifted far from His ways.

We all have busy lives with lots of reasons for taking those Glasses off. "I'm too tired." "I've got too much to do! I don't have time to read God's Word!" "I don't have time to go to church— how on earth will I get the laundry done?" "Man, when I get home from work, I just need to zone out in front of the television." Yuck! Those kinds of attitudes can wreak havoc on our relationship with God and make it difficult to hear His voice. But don't faint! Press on! Ask Him how you can rearrange your schedule so you can stay in close relationship with Him. He will be happy to show you! *Let us not become weary in doing good, for*

at the proper time we will reap a harvest if we do not give up."
(Galatians 6:9)

There may be other reasons you don't want to wear your God Glasses. They may pinch your nose. It takes effort and sometimes it's uncomfortable to do things that are in our best interest, but the long-term benefits and rewards greatly outweigh whatever we might perceive as the moment's adversity or discomfort.

In nearly every area of life, there is a price to pay for success. In academics if you want to earn a degree, you must attend classes, study, complete the assignments, and pass the tests. In finance if you want to be debt free, you must not spend more than you earn. In relationships if you want to have friends, you must show yourself friendly to people. In agricultural, you must plant your crop if you expect a harvest.

None of us have difficulty understanding these concepts because they are pretty easy to understand. Jesus taught people this way. In Matthew 13:18-23, the parable of the Sower helps us discover the key for seeing desired results in our own lives. *"Listen then to what the parable of the sower means: When anyone hears the message about the kingdom and does not understand it, the evil one comes and snatches away what was sown in his heart. This is the seed sown along the path. The one who received the seed that fell on rocky places is the man who hears the word and at once receives it with joy. But since he has no root, he lasts only a short time. When trouble or persecution comes because of the word, he quickly falls away. The one who received the seed that fell among the thorns is the man who hears the word, but the worries of this life and the deceitfulness of wealth choke it, making it unfruitful. But the one who received the seed that fell on good soil is the man who hears the word and understands it. He produces a crop, yielding a hundred, sixty or thirty times what was sown."*

As you read that, did you notice who doesn't succeed? That's right—it's the person who quits! The person who says, "I just don't feel like it. I'm too tired." In other words, the person who takes off his God Glasses because they irritate his nose, who chooses not to persevere and ends up stumbling because he can no longer see clearly. Choosing God's way of thinking and seeing is great as long as everything is going well, but when discomfort and trouble arrive, many people depart from *The Way* and choose their way: the *wrong* way.

Another reason some people may choose not to wear their God Glasses is because they've allowed them to become smeared and dirty, giving a cloudy view of the situation and distorting truth. In a day when there is considerable debate of its existence, the Bible still tells us there *is* absolute truth. These are the words of Jesus Himself, found in John 14:6 (AMP): *"...I am the Way and the Truth and the Life..."* But if we muddy our lenses with half-truths of the world, our Glasses become unclean because we no longer have the absolute truth in our hearts.

Many times what we believe as truth was planted in our minds by well-intentioned parents, ministers, and friends, or may have come from books, television, or the internet. However, some of what we learned may not be truth at all, but rather, traditions we embraced because of our deep-rooted feelings for the people who taught us, or because we believe if something can be found in print, presented on television, or repeated over and over on the internet—it must be true! Sometimes it can be a painful process,·

both internally and externally, to confront untruth. *"Making the Word of God of no effect through your tradition which you have handed down. And many such things you do."* (Mark 7:13 NKJ) As we read Jesus' words, we must ask ourselves whether our traditions have made the Word of God incapable of producing good results in our lives.

One such tradition I personally had to confront was the belief that I had to be "good" to go to heaven. On the surface that may appear to be the truth, but closer scrutiny will reveal that it is not. If your thought process is the same as mine was in this example, then your glasses are smeared and the Word of God is of no effect. Bear with me a moment as I try to explain. Belief in Jesus—the Truth—and the price He paid on our behalf is, in fact, the one and *only* way to heaven!

We've discussed the price Jesus paid for all of us to be a part of His family. It isn't our sin that will keep any of us *out* of heaven and our good deeds will not get any of us *into* heaven. The determining factor is not about behavior. It is our answer to this simple question: "Do you believe in Jesus?"

If this is difficult to accept, perhaps you need to check your Glasses against God's Word to be sure they aren't smeared or dirty with the traditions (false beliefs) of men. There is truth and it is found in God's Word. Read it, absorb it, grow in it, and be set free from the traditions of men. There are many, many traditions that blur our vision. I encourage you to embrace the whole Word with an open heart and clean God Glasses. God has done so very much for you and wants you to benefit from all of it.

Let's pretend now that you are in financial debt and I know

all of your pertinent financial information. One day, I decide that because I love you so dearly, I will contact the bank and pay all of your debts for you. Now, if you don't know I have paid your debts in full, you will still continue to pay the bank. That would be no benefit to you, but when someone tells you your debts have been paid, you will be one very happy camper, won't you? Will you continue sending monthly payments to the bank if you find out you are debt free? I don't think so!

This is a small and unworthy comparison in reference to the great price Jesus paid for us, but I hope you get the point. Jesus came and paid the debt for all the wrong you would ever do so you could be with Him for eternity. Good works are not your ticket to this new life. They are a result of it. Even so, good works do have a place in our lives. When we understand that Jesus paid our debt in full, good works are a sincere and very natural outgrowth of that realization. Doing good works becomes our nature as we seek to honor God. They can bring us joy, fulfillment, and purpose, but they will not bring us eternal life with God. The gift of eternal life is just that: a *gift*. You can't earn it and you can't lose it. You receive it by faith. This is the most freeing news of a lifetime!

If you are seeking the truth, then come now in faith to receive Jesus. He will reward you because your faith pleases Him. *"But without faith it is impossible to please Him, for he who comes to God must believe that He is, and that He is a rewarder of those who diligently seek Him."* (Hebrews 11:6 NKJ)

A favorite Scripture of mine is Ephesians 2:8-9. *"For it is by grace you have been saved, through faith—and this not from yourselves, it is the gift of God—not by works, so that no one can boast."* Doesn't reading those verses feel good? We have been saved "not as a result of works, so that no one may boast." That's my favorite part. It's not because of what we *do*. If it was, then some people may feel justified thinking, "Well, of course I'm going to heaven. I have just been *so wonderful*! I have been kind to everybody. ...Well, *pretty* kind to most people, but *mostly kind* to everybody. So, sure, I'm going to heaven!" But it doesn't work that way. Not one of us can take credit for our salvation—it's a gift by grace through faith. We receive God's free gift based on what Jesus did for us. It's settled.

Not too long ago, my daughter, Jill, gave me a pair of expensive sunglasses she had purchased for herself while in London. They were simply stunning. I had been playfully pestering her to give me the sunglasses because I liked them so much, but it had all been in fun. I certainly never expected her to actually take me seriously! When she told me she wanted me to have them, I didn't want to take them. They were much too valuable and she had paid a very high price for them. They were *hers*, not mine! After much debate, I reluctantly received the precious gift she wanted to give me. I treasured those sunglasses because I knew they had been given to me with genuine love. To my surprise, however, I couldn't bring myself to use them. Instead, I tucked them safely in a drawer so they wouldn't get lost or damaged and I continued to rely on my "five dollar specials" whenever the need arose. The London sunglasses were just too valuable to use from my perspective! Eventually, Jill noticed and began encouraging me to use her gift, freely and joyfully.

That is what we do sometimes with the gift of salvation the

Lord has given us. With a very high price, the highest ever paid in history, God gave us His only begotten Son, Jesus, as a gift to be used. Through Jesus, we can live fully and completely without worry, doubt, or fear. If we will put on our God Glasses and look intently, studying God's Word, we will see clearly, without smears or blurred vision, without the distortion of tradition.

You have a pair of God Glasses with a prescription specifically designed to meet all of your needs. They fit you perfectly, provide clear vision, look stunning with every piece of your wardrobe, and suit every single occasion. So go ahead, put on your God Glasses.

Oh …you look awesome!

THE IDEA IS NOT TO GET THE WORD OUT, BUT TO LET THE WORD OUT.

–DICK RASANEN

two

what does
GOD LOOK LIKE?

Have you ever wondered what God looks like? Some people think God looks like Charlton Heston, the star of the Hollywood movie classic, *The Ten Commandments*. Others imagine God as blond and frail based on artist's renderings they've seen in art galleries. But if you really want to get an accurate picture of God, all you need to do is open your Bible and put on your God Glasses. Did you know He really wants you to *know* Him?

God desires a personal, one-on-one relationship with you. The way to do that is to spend time with Him. As you develop your relationship with Him through His Word and by talking with Him in prayer, God promises His seemingly hidden attributes will become clearer as He begins to reveal His character and nature to you personally.

God *is* love. He is perfect and good *all* the time! Everything about Him is awesome and beautiful. If you can't see Him that way yet, sorrow, trauma, or tragedy may be blocking your view.

You may believe that God is the One who allowed the pain and loss in your life, or worse yet, that He actually caused it. That is exactly what Satan wants you to believe. His job is to kill, steal, and destroy—and he takes his job very seriously. As the father of lies, he is more than happy to wreak havoc in our lives, all the while pointing his crooked finger at God so we will think that God is the one responsible for our pain.

Many Christians proclaim that God is sovereign and can do whatever He wants. The word sovereign means monarch, King, or Supreme Ruler with sovereign power and authority. That sounds like God, doesn't it? It is true He is King and has sovereign power and authority. I agree 100 percent! But let's take a closer look. If we place human attributes on our Sovereign God, we may make the mistake of assuming His motives are comparable with our fleshly ones. There are good rulers and there are tyrants. He is neither. He is perfectly good all the time! He never lies, steals, or destroys—that's the other guy!

Psalm 68:20 tells us God is a God who saves and from Him comes escape from death. Numbers 23:19 says, *"God is not a man, that He should lie, nor a son of man, that He should change His mind. Does He speak and then not act? Does He promise and not fulfill?"*

God has promised you salvation in accordance with His will. In Acts 4:12 (NAS), Peter cries out to us about who Jesus is. *"And there is salvation in no one else; for there is no other name under heaven that has been given among men by which we must be saved."* Jesus is the only way to heaven. God will not alter His perfect plan of salvation. He will not change His mind or reconsider His own design. *"For no matter how many promises God has made, they are*

"Yes" in Christ..." (2 Corinthians 1:20) Now that's reassuring news! Psalm 138:2 (NKJ) says, *"...For You have magnified Your Word above all Your name."* God's integrity is beyond reproach. You can trust Him completely because He only wants good things for you.

My dad was a great man and a lot of fun to be around. One thing I knew for certain about my dad was that his word was his word, as good as gold, and once given, would never be taken back. When I was a teenager, if I asked him if I could borrow the car on a Friday night and he said yes, I knew I could make plans with my friends with confidence because on Friday night that car was mine! I never had to worry about him changing his mind because he was not a double-minded man.

How much more valuable are the promises of our heavenly Father! Whatever God says, He holds to it. If He said it, He won't violate it. He simply can't go against His own nature. He is incapable of denying Himself, His Word, or His promises. We would have a very hard time putting our faith in God if He didn't keep His promises. It's hard to believe anyone who changes their mind or takes back their promises whenever they feel like it. Being double-minded and fickle are human traits, *not* God's!

God's ways far surpass our own human frailties. *"'For My thoughts are not your thoughts, nor are your ways My ways,' says the Lord. 'For as the heavens are higher than the earth, so are My ways higher than your ways, and My thoughts than your thoughts.'"* (Isaiah 55:8-9 NKJ) As we draw closer to Him through the Word and in prayer, we will start seeing what He is doing and then we can ask Him if we can be a part of it. What a joy to participate in His perfect plans! If we devise our own plan for ourselves based on our imperfect human wisdom and power and then think that we can expect Him to bless it, well, it's probably not going to turn out the way we had hoped. Oh, He'll let us try. In His great love for us, He will let us try. But He will also wait patiently for us to notice that we've got the whole thing backwards! When we wear our God Glasses to see what He is doing and then ask if we can be a part of it, He will let us know what is best for us and He will bless us with that sovereign plan.

When we rely solely on our own reasoning and allow traditions of men to guide us through life's circumstances, we can arrive at conclusions totally contrary to His plan for us. We should never expect God to give us the thumbs up when we come up with a new way of doing things, imposing our actions on His plan.

It is nearly impossible to live on this planet without being slammed daily with a barrage of messages that conflict with the truth of God's Word. Although His ways are higher than our ways, we can still fall in the trap of believing what the world presents to us as truth. There are people under the tragic delusion that we all pray to the same god—we just have different names for him and different ways to pray to him. Believing this lie means Buddha, Allah, and Jesus are the same, therefore any and all who are called "God" will lead them to heaven, as long as false gods are worshipped with sincerity. How this must grieve our Lord.

"For there is one God and one Mediator between God and men, the Man Christ Jesus." (1 Timothy 2:5 NKJ) This is a very important truth to grasp. When we put our faith and trust in Jesus and His Word, He will bring it to pass. *"Heaven and earth will pass away, but My words will never pass away."* (Matthew 24:35)

It may feel a bit foreign to think this way because most things in life seem to change constantly, but just because someone hasn't experienced truth doesn't mean it doesn't exist! You don't have to touch a live wire to know electricity is real. We can turn on a lamp to see light. In the same way, we can turn on the truth of God's Word and see light inside our hearts. We can choose to take a chance on God's uncompromising integrity and enjoy new levels of love, honesty, and trust in our lives. He is Almighty God and what He says He will do, He will do.

How do we know whether our view of who God is, is correct or not? Simple. We look through our God Glasses. That's why He gave them to us. If our way of thinking doesn't match up with who He says He is in His Word, then we are looking at Him through the wrong lenses!

In an era when everyone seems to question everything, it's funny how few seem to ever question their beliefs about God, as though to do so would be blasphemous, somehow off-limits. God is confident about who He is. He is not worried about His reputation and is not concerned if you examine your beliefs against the truth of His Word. He can take the scrutiny. He *wants* you to know the truth about Him. He *wants* you to decide what you believe so you will be confident in the truth and it will set you free. So go ahead, put on your God Glasses. Look closely at His face and be blessed! *"But the man who looks intently into the perfect law that gives freedom, and continues to do this, not forgetting what he has heard, but doing it—he will be blessed in what he does."* (James 1:25)

This may come as a shock to you but not everything that happens in life is God's will. Although some may falsely believe it, He is not some master puppeteer in the sky, cruelly pulling the strings of our lives, and we are not His marionettes totally devoid of choice! We live in a corrupt world and each of us has the privilege of making right and wrong choices. Good or bad, more often than not, those choices not only affect us, but other people as well.

You have probably heard it said that everything happens for a reason. I believed that for many years. It was easy for me to think that way. If God was in charge of everything, it put all the responsibility and blame on God for whatever happened in my life: the good, the bad, the ugly, the evil, and the indifferent. It was all Him and *His* doing. Since He was in charge of everything, then everything, including evil, must have originated with Him. That was what I believed before I put on my God Glasses. Once I put them on, I was able to receive and believe what God said in His Word to me, and about me. Finally I realized the great love He had for me. "*Because he has loved Me, therefore I will deliver him; I will set him securely on high, because he has known My name.*" (Psalm 91:14 NAS)

My new understanding of Him and His great love for me changed my perspective forever. Suddenly when I started looking at my circumstances through my God Glasses, I could see my life more clearly. I realized that the events of my life were not always God's will for me. Now that was a life-changing moment! There should have been a street sign on the road of my life that read: Huge turn ahead! Buckle up! You're in for a wild, amazing ride with Jesus!

As you travel through life and you come to a fork in the road, you can choose the right path—potholes, obstacles, and all—or like Jonah, who found himself in the belly of a whale, you can choose to go in the exact opposite direction believing with self-determination that a smooth, comfortable ride is in store. It's really up to you and how you will choose.

God does have a purpose for your life and it starts with choosing Jesus as King in your life. "*The Lord is not slow in keeping His promise, as some understand slowness. He is patient with you, not wanting anyone to perish, but everyone to come to repentance.*" (2 Peter 3:9) He does not want anyone to die without first knowing Jesus. His will is for us to be in heaven with Him because He loves each of us so dearly. Sadly, some still die without making the choice that guarantees eternal life with Him.

The Lord proclaims to the world through Scripture that He loves us and desires good and not calamity for us. So why are some so dull of hearing and unmotivated to choose Him? Because somewhere along the road they have believed lies that sound something like, "I'm a good person. If God wants me to be in heaven, I will be in heaven." Or, "If God wants me to be poor and sick, well, it is just His will." NOT! Satan must get pretty cocky when he hears someone speak words like that. If anybody spoke evil of our spouse or best friend the way many people malign the character of God, we would be outraged! The truth is, God promises to cause everything to work together for our good because we love Him and we are called according to His purpose. (See Romans 8:28.) In other words, God can make delicious lemonade out of any rotten lemons the devil throws at us.

God gives us the freedom to choose or reject Him. He gives us free will in everything. Deuteronomy 11:26-27 (NAS) says,

"See, I am setting before you today a blessing and a curse: the blessing, if you listen to the commandments of the Lord your God, which I am commanding you today." The way we live is a choice. In fact, there are life and death situations around us all the time. We can choose either to apply ourselves to tasks and accomplishments or we can choose to be lazy and avoid them. We can sleep late or rise early. We are faced with decision making on a daily basis. Thankfully, most decisions are simple choices with no life-altering implications. Even so, there are times when we are confronted with decisions that can completely alter the course of our lives for the better or worse.

The decision whether or not to ingest illegal drugs is a good example here. The choice we make will have direct and sometimes immediate consequences that can positively or horrifically affect our lives. What if we buy into the lie that we are the one and only human being in the *entire world* who can do drugs without negative consequences? What if we succumb to peer pressure and choose to go ahead and take the risk, which results in an overdose and we die? Whose responsibility is it? Ours or God's? It's pretty easy to see that it is not God's will for any of us to die as a result of doing drugs. If we put our faith in Jesus and let Him lead us in the way we should go, our course will not be one of random chance but rather one filled with abundant life and goodness that Jesus died to give us.

God has given you a role in making His wonderful plans and purposes come to pass in your life. When you put on your God Glasses and look into God's Word, you will see the road map you've been looking for that reveals the path you are to take. Look at Psalm 119:105: *"Your Word is a lamp to my feet, and a light for my path."* Don't you want to walk in that light? I know I do! I want to be a "doer" of the Word and not just a "hearer." Before we can hear and do, however, we have to *know* the Truth so we don't hear and do something *un*truthful. If we're going to put our trust in God, we've got to know what the truth is. Otherwise we might believe lies, making His Word ineffective in our lives.

Let's take a look at some of Jesus' familiar words in Matthew 6:9-10 (NAS) when He tells His disciples how they should pray. *"Pray, then, in this way: 'Our Father who is in heaven, hallowed be Your name. Your kingdom come Your will be done, on earth as it is in heaven.'"* Jesus instructs His disciples to pray God's will be done on earth just like it is in heaven. He is teaching us to pray that what happens in heaven will also happen here on earth. Why would Jesus teach us to pray that way? Could it be that He wants us to understand we have a hand in His outcome? I believe so!

When you trust God with your life, you make the most important decision of all: choosing Jesus as your Lord and Savior. Once you do that, you can look through your God Glasses at your life circumstances and let your choices correspond with God's will.

You may be thinking, "But you don't know what I've experienced in my life! You don't know the tragedies I've suffered. God could have stopped them, if He had wanted." There aren't always answers for life's circumstances, but we can know one thing: God doesn't send evil. He will not kill, steal, or destroy. Even in the worst circumstances, we are still responsible for our attitudes and responses. We can choose to walk in faith, believing God for the best possible outcome and knowing He will be with us every step of the way, or we can let our difficult circumstances overtake us by holding on to our anger, becoming bitter, and holding God responsible for what happened to us.

When terrible things happen and tragedy strikes, the questions we need to ask are: "Lord, how do you want me to respond to this? How can I draw closer to you?" Rather than asking, "Why is this happening to me?" Even if we don't have the answers to our "why" questions when something awful happens, we can always know God is perfectly good and the devil is pure evil. This may seem too simple to be true, but it is true! Anything good and abundant comes from God. Anything destructive is from the devil. For me that's a no-brainer because John 10:10 (NAS) says, *"The thief comes only to steal and kill and destroy; I came that they may have life, and have it abundantly."* Look at what is written in James 1:17. *"Every good and perfect gift is from above, coming down from the Father of the heavenly lights, who does not change like shifting shadows."*

God is the Restorer, the Redeemer and the One who will lead you and guide you in truth so you can avoid the enemy's traps. God will not go back on His Word and has told us in Deuteronomy 30:19 to choose life! *"This day I call heaven and earth as witnesses against you that I have set before you life and death, blessings and curses. Now choose life, so that you and your children may live."*

Disease entered the world when Adam and Eve chose to disobey God in the Garden. Their sinful choice affects us to this day. It was never God's will for people to suffer. That's why He sent Jesus so we could be free from this curse.

"Who will bring any charge against those whom God has chosen? It is God who justifies." (Romans 8:33) If you place your life in

Jesus' hands, He declares you "Not Guilty" and claims you as His own child, setting you free! None of us are good enough to go to heaven in our own right, but by receiving the free gift of salvation through Jesus, we are no longer guilty. We are made right with God. When you realize God loves you unconditionally—not because you've behaved well, or prayed a lot, or read your Bible, but because Jesus has paid the price for you to be free from spiritual punishment for all the things you have ever done—you can experience true freedom. God says, "I have put My Spirit on the inside of you." That's for eternity! Follow Christ and you will have your very own pair of God Glasses.

Go to God's Word and discover Him for who He really is. Find out all about Him. He is the best friend you will ever have. He is the One who sticks closer to you than a brother. He will never leave you or forget about you.

People may have betrayed you or let you down in the past, sharing secrets you've told them, but God won't. Every whisper you've made to Him and every treasured thought you've shared with Him, stays with Him. He will never let you down. He can be trusted.

When you get a clear picture of how much God loves you and absorb it into your heart, you will not only look at yourself differently but you will see others differently too. You can discover the depth, breath, height, and width of His love as you spend time with Him praying and reading His Word. If you seek Him a lot, you'll know Him more intimately. If you seek Him a little, you'll only know Him a little. God won't force you to draw closer to Him but He is inviting you. The sooner you spend time getting to know Him, the sooner you will reap the benefits. God's Word is food for your spirit. Read it with your eyes, hear it with your ears, and practice saying it with your mouth. Allow it to transform your life today. Put on your God Glasses!

GOD HAS PROMISED TO KEEP HIS PEOPLE, AND HE WILL KEEP HIS PROMISE.

–CHARLES SPURGEON

three

seeing yourself as
GOD SEES YOU

3

Have you ever seen a candid photo of yourself and been surprised by what you saw? Usually we have a better image in our minds than what our eyes actually confront us with! While carnival mirrors are amusing, they can make us look tall, short, skinny, or chubby, but we are expecting distortion when we peer into one. A candid photo, however, can sometimes be a real shocker! Is that how I *really* look?

A couple of years ago while I was in a let's-shed-some-unwanted-pounds kind of mood, I signed up with a local weight loss center. During my first routine weigh-in, I noticed a mirror placed strategically in front of the scale. Oh, it was such a *good* mirror! It made me look nice and skinny and I so appreciated the distortion. *Brother*, did I look good! I knew what I saw in the mirror wasn't really me yet, but what I saw encouraged me to press toward my weight loss goal. I knew if I finished my course that I would eventually look like that in real life. I wanted to be the person I saw in that mirror.

Did you know God has created a spiritual mirror for you? It's better than any natural mirror you will ever find. His mirror allows you to see yourself the way He sees you. Using His mirror gives you His perspective on you, which is the right perspective. Put on your God Glasses right now as we look at what the Word says about His mirror: *"For if anyone is a hearer of the Word and not a doer, he is like a man observing his natural face in a mirror; for he observes himself, goes away, and immediately forgets what kind of man he was. But he who looks into the perfect law of liberty and continues in it, and is not a forgetful hearer but a doer of the work, this one will be blessed in what he does."* (James 1:23-25 NKJ)

God's Word is a mirror to us. He gave us His mirror so we can see how we really look from His perspective. As our Creator, wouldn't He have the correct image of us? Problems come if we don't look into His mirror to find out who we really are. Instead, we hold on to the image of our old self that was developed in the past.

Many of us carry distorted images of ourselves based on our past relationships, experiences, and behavior. Some of those images are so warped you would think we do live at the carnival, but nothing could be further from the truth! What we see is something totally different from God's mirror. We choose to believe what we see in our own mirror based on what we have gone through, rather than the true image of ourselves found in God's mirror.

Have you been condemning yourself because you can't seem to do anything right for more than two hours, much less two days? Join the rest of us! We all seem to be members of that club. Many of us messed up last week, last night, and again first thing this morning. We aren't perfect. If we were, we wouldn't need Jesus. When we compare ourselves to Jesus, who was without sin, we fall far short of the mark no matter how good we try to be. We are so convinced that Jesus is sizing up our performance, it's no wonder we beat ourselves up. Good news! He isn't sizing us up. He's looking for a heart to follow Him.

This would be a great time to get your God Glasses out. You're going to need them.

The more we know God and the closer we want to be to Him, the more our imperfections become evident to us. Before we even realize it, we can kick into performance mode: more praying, more Bible study, more nice—far nicer than any of our friends and family. But the minute we slip up in any area, we condemn ourselves. Are you still wearing your God Glasses? Good! Now look in the mirror. Do you see the beautiful object of God's affection? The Bible says you were made in His image. God looks at you and sees the image of His Son on the inside of you. "Beautiful," He says.

Would you ever deliberately be unkind to someone? Call them fat? Tell them they can't do anything right? In your heart of hearts, you wouldn't want to treat anyone like that because you know Jesus loves them so much He died for them. Well, one day the Lord spoke to my heart—not in words I could hear, but in the voice my heart understood. He asked, "Would you ever be intentionally hateful to someone?" I said, "No Lord, of course not." "Why?" He asked. I proceeded to tell Him. "Because You love every one of them. You died for them. I want to love those You love." I waited for His response. Then He said, "Why are you so hateful toward yourself? I died for you, too." I had never seen it like that before! I figured it was okay for me to say and think bad things about myself. It had never occurred to me that I counted among those I was to love.

God gave me this message that day: "Love God. Love others. Love yourself." Now my God Glasses help me see myself as God does. I matter to Him. I count! He isn't keeping score of my behavior. He is enamored by my heart, a heart made in His image and likeness. God is love. He loves me and He loves you. It's the devil that wants you to be cruel to yourself, speaking words of condemnation and ridicule.

Your life experiences up to this point may have painted a rather ugly portrait of you that can seem nearly impossible to erase. For some people, it may seem as though it has been painted with permanent ink. Guess what? That image can be wiped away as easily as removing dry erase marker from a white board. If you make the choice to look intently at God's Word with your God Glasses on, you will have a new image and an accurate view of yourself. That's great news! You need to believe what you read in His Word.

Just glancing at the Word won't create a lasting image. Take the time to really meditate on it, get it deep down into your heart. I promise you will really like the new image you see of yourself.

When I was younger, hateful words were spoken to me. I was told I was a lazy, good-for-nothing person who would never amount to anything. I'm sure you'll agree how sad that is. No child should ever be told that. Because that person was an adult and I was a child, I believed what they said to me was true. That poor self-image stayed with me, even as I grew up, but it was very different from the truth in the Bible. What I didn't know was that God already had a plan to make things right in my life.

"For I know the plans I have for you," declares the Lord, *"plans to prosper you and not to harm you, plans to give you hope and a future."* (Jeremiah 29:11)

Once I asked Jesus into my heart and to be my best friend, I began seeing who I really was with all my strengths and abilities. As I studied His Word, I found these Scriptures that showed me His truth: *"I can do everything through Him who gives me strength."* (Philippians 4:13); *"...If God is for us, who can be against us?"* (Romans 8:31) and, *"Yet in all these things we are more than conquerors through Him who loved us."* (Romans 8:37 NKJ)

I started seeing myself the way God sees me. The more I discovered the truth, the more my life changed and my condemning thoughts of failure had to leave me. The list of Scriptures that show each of us who we are in Christ goes on and on. The way I see myself now is quite freeing and significantly different from the way I saw myself before I gave my heart to Jesus.

Freedom comes with the truth and bondage comes with lies. The Holy Spirit can change you from the inside out, but first you have to believe it is possible. I encourage you to go to the mirror of God's Word and let this miraculous transformation take place in your life. In John 8:31-32, Jesus tells us to hold fast to His teaching in order to be free. You must continue in it, which means not vacillating between two views. By doing God's Word, looking at it, and continuing to live in it, you will keep your God Glasses on and see yourself the way God sees you.

We all want to be set free from wrong thinking. We need to decide to just flat-out believe God's Word if we are ever going to get to the peaceful place He has for us. Of course, almost everything is harder when you first start out. Just ask anyone who begins a new diet or exercise program. Better yet, ask a new parent. They can tell you what hard work is!

If you start out with the attitude, "I'm going to believe God no matter what," you will not be alone. The Holy Spirit will be with you. He's called the Helper because that's His job: to help you. Nothing will give Him more joy than seeing you succeed in God's plans and purposes.

No matter how your self-image got distorted, it affects your perception of your value. Perhaps it wasn't distorted by the words someone spoke about you. It may have come when bad things happened to you. Painful experiences growing up can cause you not to like yourself, making it hard for you to believe that God would actually love you. Painful memories can prevent you from seeing yourself as God sees you.

Do you know what He sees when He looks at you? He sees someone He's crazy in love with. His heart beats wildly for you! God sent His only son Jesus to die in your place so you could be with Him forever and He could lavish His great love and blessings on you.

Romans 3:23 tells us, *"For all have sinned and fall short of the glory of God."* We fall short of God's glory because of sin. Since God is holy, He can't overlook sin. That's why He provided a solution for our sins so we would not have to be separated from Him forever. That solution is Jesus.

There is a wonderful translation of Romans 5:16 in the Today's English Version Bible. It says, *"And there is a difference between God's gift and the sin of one man. After the one sin came judgment of guilty, but after so many sins comes the undeserved gift of not guilty."* God has declared you not guilty! When you come to Jesus, tell Him you are sorry for your past. Receive His free gift of forgiveness and restored relationship. Then you have no past. You are a new creation in Him. Old things are passed away and He makes all things new. No matter where you have come from or what you have done, God declares you *not guilty*. Isn't that incredible news?

Let's look at some more wonderful promises from the Father to you: *"As far as the east is from the west, so far has He removed our transgressions from us."* (Psalm 103:12); *"I, even I, am He who blots out your transgressions, for My own sake, and remembers your sins no more."* (Isaiah 43:25); and *"Who will accuse God's chosen people? God Himself declares them not guilty!"* (Romans 8:33 GNT)

We can pile up guilt upon guilt, can't we? Sometimes we are so ashamed of ourselves that instead of running to God, we run away from Him. That's tragic. Did you know that when you say you are sorry and turn from your old life, God doesn't even remember it anymore? When you get right with God, you can walk free of any guilt that may have plagued you in the past. So, don't run from God; run straight into His arms. He's the only One who can truly make your life right. He's not going to hold your past against you or punish you for anything you've done wrong. This world we live in delivers consequences for poor choices, but God will totally forgive and not hold anything against us.

God does not want us to kick ourselves for our shortcomings. He wants us to see ourselves in Jesus, who provides everything we need to be the person He created us to be. Get rid of your distorted self-hating images. They can hinder you from becoming all God wants you to be. Here's the proof: *"But if we confess our sins to God, He will keep His promise and do what is right: He will forgive us our sins and purify us from all our wrongdoing."* (1 John 1:9 TEV); and *"For you died, and your life is now hidden with Christ in God."* (Colossians 3:3)

You might be thinking "Great! I can do anything I want and God won't even care!" But understanding God's goodness does not give us a license to sin. It gives us a reason and desire not to. Though none of us is capable of living a perfectly sinless life, we should always make it our aim to live a life in which God would be pleased.

Let's look at Psalm 103:11-14 (NAS) to understand more of how God sees. *"For as high as the heavens are above the earth, so great is His loving kindness toward those who fear Him. As far as the east is from the west, so far has He removed our transgressions from us. Just as a father has compassion on his children, so the Lord has compassion on those who fear Him. For He Himself knows our frame; He is mindful that we are but dust."*

What a beautiful picture of how God sees you! He not only forgave your sins when you confessed them, He also put them as far as the east is from the west. Now that's pretty far! As a matter of fact, it's so far it can't be measured. Does this mean that everything you do from now on will be perfect? Of course not! Only One has ever been perfect. It certainly wasn't me and it won't be you. It was Jesus. God is for you, not against you. He looks at Jesus inside your heart, knows you belong to Him, and accepts you.

Did you know that if you travel the earth from the north to the south and keep going, when you reach the southern-most point you will begin to travel north again, but when you go east, you will never begin to go west? It can't be done. That's what the Lord is saying. He has put our sins so far from us, they cannot even be measured! How great is that? And He says, "I don't remember them." He doesn't remember them? Our limited human minds can't even comprehend that thought, but He is God and He is faithful to do what He says in His Word. So when we wake up with a case of the guilties over something we did in the past but have already confessed to God, He says, "Sorry again? For what? I don't remember what you're talking about." He forgave us when we confessed our sin. It's over. His mercies are new every morning.

He has equipped you to be the person He created you to be. He has equipped you through every promise He has provided for you in His Word. He has even given you a pair of God Glasses so you can see yourself the way He sees you. He doesn't want you to lay your Glasses down, look into a natural mirror and say, "I don't like what I see. I don't like anything about me." He wants you to put those Glasses on, look at your image in His mirror and say to yourself, "I have Jesus in me. I am great. I am awesome. I am beautiful." When you do this, you will be speaking the truth.

In Romans 8:31, it says, *"...If God is for us, who can be against us?"* Think about that. If God is for you, what difference does it make what people say about you? It certainly isn't God saying those things. Don't be shaken by circumstances. Be moved by the Word of God and then move forward with Him.

Let His truth determine your future. Let it color the pages of your life. Take hold of all the promises He's spoken over you and agree with Him, placing your faith in His faithfulness. Begin speaking aloud what God says about you in His Word and then watch your world change as you paint the canvas of your beautiful future with Him.

GOD LOVES US THE WAY WE ARE, BUT HE LOVES US TOO MUCH TO LEAVE US THAT WAY.

–LEIGHTON FORD

four

seeing others as
GOD SEES THEM

4

Let's face it, dealing with difficult people is not easy! Anyone who's ever made a frantic call to tech support knows what I am talking about. It goes something like this: you call the tech support hotline and start counting the rings. After the eighth or ninth ring you lose count as your anxiety rises. You tell your tale of woe to the first monotone voice that finally answers, who then transfers you to another person, who transfers you to another, and another. Each time you have to restate your reason for calling, until you "accidently" get disconnected after you, in exasperation, ask to speak with a supervisor. Wearing your God Glasses will help you deal with people the way God wants you to—even in less than desirable circumstances—and even when you can't see them on the other end of the phone.

Do you think we see people the way God does? Let's examine some of what His Word has to say about the subject:

First Samuel 16:7 (NKJ) says, "...*For the Lord does not see as man sees; for man looks at the outward appearance, but the Lord looks at the heart."* God makes it clear He doesn't see people as we see them. We tend to form opinions about others by looking at the outward appearance *especially* if we aren't wearing our God Glasses. For instance, if a person has a good job, wears nice clothes and appears to have a prosperous life, we might assume they are successful and all is right with the world for them. What we see on the outside may not always be the truth, however. That person could be in extreme debt, have lots of destructive relationships, or have addictions that aren't easily recognized by the naked eye. We judge according to what we see in appearance and actions, but God looks at the *heart*. It's what's on the *inside* of a person that counts with Him.

With our God Glasses on, we have the ability to see what God sees that we could not otherwise. They give us the ability to see people from His perspective through His eyes of love. Without our God Glasses, we may look at people critically or judgmentally, mislabeling them as failures or losers based on what we see on the outside. But God sees them as successful and as winners because He knows He has good plans for their lives. We, on the other hand, might view others' negative circumstances and size them up, thinking, "They're on a downward spiral. Things will never get any better with them." In John 3:16, however, God tells us He loves *everyone* so much, He sent His Son Jesus to save us. We need His perspective because it helps us see others as He sees them and helps us avoid criticizing and judging others.

A look into the Book of Romans makes God's perspective even clearer. *"But God demonstrates His own love for us in this: While we were still sinners, Christ died for us."* (Romans 5:8) God demonstrated His love for us, not when we were perfect and deserved it, but while we were yet sinners in our worst possible condition!

You may be thinking, "I wasn't even born when Jesus came to earth. I hadn't committed any sins yet!" Jesus paid the price for the sins of the whole world. The great price He paid was all-inclusive, covering the sins of the past, present, and future. Our debts are paid in full, no matter how you look at it. That's how fully and completely God demonstrates His love for us.

So, what is it that can make people so irritating to us? Why do we let what they do and say get on our last nerve? Because they are people just like us and as much as we hate to admit it, we are just as capable of getting on other peoples nerves sometimes too! Let's choose right now to do unto others as we would have them do unto us. Let's choose to see them through the unfailing, love-filled eyes of God.

Some people have God Glasses that are cracked and damaged. Perhaps you have a pair like that. Have past hurts or offenses caused you so much pain you have a hard time clearly seeing another person's heart? Unforgiveness and unhealed wounds and offenses make it very difficult to give someone else a break, distorting and warping the view seen through damaged lenses that are in desperate need of God's healing adjustment. He wants you to see clearly. He wants to heal your sight. He wants your Glasses properly repaired and adjusted so your relationships can be restored.

Some people appear to have God Glasses that are in good condition. They might seem to see clearly but they are just pretending. Actually, they are wearing glasses without lenses that attempt to mimic the ones God wants them to use. These are the people who act differently when they are at church than they do in everyday life. You may even know a few people like this. We call people who say one thing but act another, hypocrites. Their outward attitude seems right but their heart attitude doesn't line up. There are many Christians who are just going through the motions, putting on a front, going to church, saying all the right things—even using church lingo, but their hearts aren't right. Looking at them, you might think they are very loving toward others, but what's their motive? Just too look good? Man looks at outward appearance but God looks at the heart.

When we look at the outward appearance of a person like this, we may think, "I want to be like them." But the well-polished frames you see on the outside don't necessarily reflect what's on the inside. Matthew 15:8 says, *"These people honor Me with their lips, but their hearts are far from Me."* It's a good reminder of "what you see is not always what you get." God Glasses have special lenses. You can't get the benefits of seeing as God sees if you only display them as an ornament to impress others. You have to put them on and use them! We must continually submit our hearts to God, allowing His love and truth to flow through us to others, then we can see clearly!

Some people wear another kind of glasses—glasses that give them a critical, judgmental view of others. Have you ever been around someone like this? They think the worst of people and situations, rarely thinking about God's best. They will gossip about the way other people look, criticizing them for being too heavy or too thin, having an opinion about everything to do with what needs to be corrected in others, all the while justifying their cruelty by proclaiming, "I have the gift of spiritual discernment so I just *know* these things!" They will even claim to have heard it from the Lord!

The good news is none of these types of glasses are real God Glasses. God doesn't pretend to be something He's not and He's never critical of us. His ways are perfect. He always looks for the best in a person's heart. He is *always* for us, *never* against us.

A while ago, my friend and I were at a conference out of town. One afternoon we were hungry and decided to get a bite to eat. Rather than going out, we decided to eat at the hotel where the conference was being held so we could just relax and not feel rushed. When we got inside the restaurant, it was empty except for us. The waiter seated us, but he seated us at a dirty table. I couldn't understand why he sat us at the only dirty table when we were the only ones in the entire restaurant and there were clean tables all around us! I quickly pointed out that our table was dirty, whereupon he walked casually away to get a cloth to wipe it clean. To my surprise, instead of getting rid of the crumbs, he swept them onto our seats! I started to sit down and there were crumbs everywhere. The table was wet, the seats were wet and now covered in crumbs that were getting wet—and I was annoyed. It certainly didn't seem like we were going to have the relaxing lunch we had hoped for!

Just as I was about to call the waiter back to present him with his failing report card in Restaurant Service 101, my precious friend stepped in. Wearing her God Glasses, she reached out in love recognizing that he was obviously having a very difficult day. She smiled and generously thanked him for serving us. For a moment I thought I was having an out-of-body experience! Surely my friend and I must be having lunch in two different worlds! But we weren't. She was showing him the grace and mercy that filled her because she was seeing our waiter through the eyes of Jesus. Where I was only seeing wet crumbs and inconvenience, she was seeing the opportunity to walk in the love of Jesus toward a hurting man.

When I saw her loving response, I was sorry I had gotten frustrated with him. She had made the wise choice and I made a poor one. It was humbling. I was reminded we have to consciously wear our God Glasses at all times. If left to our natural tendencies, we'll go with our selfish nature. That situation made me realize where I am weak and where I need to further depend on Jesus' strength. It reminded me to make a choice daily, even hourly, to see people as God sees them—and not to judge them for what they do or don't do. God doesn't want us to bless people only after they have blessed us. He wants us to bless them whether we think they deserve it or not—at all times!

"Give, and it will be given to you. A good measure, pressed down, shaken together and running over, will be poured into your lap. For with the measure you use, it will be measured to you." (Luke 6:38)

God doesn't treat us badly (although we sometimes deserve it!). I'm very thankful for that. He looks past our mistakes and doesn't hold us accountable for things we've already said we were sorry for. He speaks to our hearts, "I love you so much. I demonstrated My love for you by sending Jesus." Remember that.

Remember His great love for you!

God doesn't look at where you are. He doesn't say, "Sorry. You don't deserve My love. I'm going to treat you the way you deserve to be treated." Instead, He zeros right in on you and looks at your heart. He loves you no matter what! Because He loves you, you not only have the ability to put on your God Glasses to see people as He sees them, but you also have the ability to see yourself just as He sees you. Thank goodness we don't have to rely on our own strength to see people the way God does! In fact, the Bible says those things that are impossible with man are possible with God.

You may think, "I can't live like that. It's so hard. I've never been treated that way, so how am I supposed to know how to treat others that way?" With God you can! In human weakness, He is made strong and will prove Himself to you when you put your trust in Him to work in your life. He has put His power inside you to do what you can't in the natural. His power resides in you through the Holy Spirit. All you have to do is call Him and He is faithful to hear and answer you. God has equipped and empowered you to live a fully pleasing and acceptable life for Him, but first you must choose to follow His leading.

Hebrews 11:30 (NAS) says we overcome by faith. When we believe God and His Word, we can overcome any situation. So starting with verse 30 through 31, let's look at Hebrews chapter 11: *"By faith the walls of Jericho fell down after they had been encircled for seven days. By faith Rahab the harlot did not perish along with those who were disobedient, after she had welcomed the spies in peace."*

Then verses 32 through 34 say, *"And what more shall I say?*

For time will fail me if I tell of Gideon, Barak, Samson, Jephthah, of David and Samuel and the prophets, who by faith conquered kingdoms, performed acts of righteousness, obtained promises, shut the mouths of lions, quenched the power of fire, escaped the edge of the sword, from weakness were made strong..."

Did you get all of this? They did tremendous exploits and great things because of the strength God put inside of them. They believed God and operated by faith. They trusted Him and He took them through incredibly hard times. That same strength and faith are available today for you, too. By His Spirit, God will help you to walk in faith as Zechariah 4:6 promises. *"...'Not by might nor by power, but by my Spirit,' says the Lord Almighty."*

Put your faith and trust in God and what His Word says. Believe that God will get you through hard times. He is an ever-present help in time of need. His unfailing love, mercy, and grace will be there to help you always. It's not always easy dealing with difficult people. God certainly understands that. (Don't forget He has all of us to deal with!) Call on God. He will be faithful to answer you and see you through to the other side of whatever it is you're going through or *whomever* it is you are dealing with. You will find His strength in your weakness.

Realizing how much God loves you gives you the strength and power to receive everything you need to love others, see them as God sees them, and treat them how He desires them to be treated. I've heard it said that hurting people hurt people. When you go to a grocery store or stop at a gas station, people are not always kind. Truthfully, sometimes they are downright rude and obnoxious even when you're trying to be nice! You may have run into people like that in your life. God asks you to look past their behavior and see them as He sees them. Give that extra measure of love to the (seemingly) undeserving. Ask them if they would like you to pray for them. Their response might surprise you—you could be the answer to their prayers!

If you can learn to ignore the outside appearance and look into the heart through the eyes of God, you'll see people as they really are: hurting. Everyone is struggling with something and has some level of pain. Pain is part of this life. As Christians, we carry inside of us the one thing that can help heal their pain and ease their burden—the unfathomable love of God, ready and willing to be given away.

Even when you interact with people who aren't treating you fairly, you can choose in that moment to forgive them. We can fall into the trap of believing we have to defend ourselves, but really, that's not true. God wants us to forgive people when they mistreat us. You don't always have to bring it to their attention. Forgiving them may seem foreign to you especially given today's culture, but that is exactly what Jesus did. He didn't take into account any wrongs.

When you find yourself dealing with a difficult person, ask God to give you something kind to say to them. He will give you the ability to love them with the same kind of love He lavishes on you. That's what God means when He says if you can recognize your weakness and admit it, He can be strong in your life. He says He resists the proud and gives grace to the humble. When you humble yourself before Him and say, "Lord, I need you" instead of "I don't need God. I'll take care of this myself," then you are in a position of receiving everything you need from God to walk through the situation you face.

God requires us to call on Him so He can move on our behalf. We can't do things in our own strength and expect the best results. When we put our God Glasses on, we will see clearly and be able to walk in the ways He wants us to walk. In order to do this, we need to spend time in God's Word. He talks to us through His Word and through prayer.

Proverbs 4:20-23 says, *"My son, pay attention to what I say; listen closely to my words. Do not let them out of your sight, keep them within your heart; for they are life to those who find them and health to a man's whole body. Above all else, guard your heart, for it is the wellspring of life."* The only way to overcome what happens in this world is to spend time with Jesus in His Word, because when you know the Truth, you are set free. When you see how God handles situations, you learn how He wants you to handle them. Don't be like the person with the cracked glasses. Don't stay in that place. God can heal your broken heart—but first you have to let Him.

A person with a wounded heart has a lot of trouble loving other people and seeing them as God sees them. You may have trouble with many people but the only common denominator is *you*. Check your Glasses. See if they are cracked. If they are, go to God. Ask Him to heal your wounded heart. Ask Him for healing and restoration in your relationships. You don't have to settle for cracked Glasses! And, if you have a pair of glasses you like wearing because you think you look good in them, trade them in for the real deal—God Glasses!

Decide today to be a doer of the Word, not just a reader of it, then you won't be judgmental toward everyone you see. The Word of God will transform you and your life. God is an awesome God and He has so much in store for you. It all begins with you calling out to Him and receiving by faith everything He has for you.

I ALWAYS PREFER TO BELIEVE THE BEST OF EVERYBODY— IT SAVES SO MUCH TROUBLE.

–RUDYARD KIPLING

five

seeing your family as
GOD SEES THEM

5

Think of your family right now. Ask yourself how you would describe them. What do you see? How do you think God sees your family? Does your view match God's view?

Relationships, especially family relationships, are a tremendous blessing from the Lord and yet they can be the most difficult challenges we face. Our family of origin, our adopted family, and the one we marry into contain complex challenges and rewards that can be hurtful or they can help us grow closer. God made us each to be a unique individual and to be part of a family unit. We carry responsibility in the family, yet we can all have different views and priorities.

Do you think God sees our family members as inconsiderate, emotional people who refuse to load the dishwasher? Does He get exasperated with their procrastination? Does He want to scream when they pick up the remote to change the channel from what we were watching? No, I don't think so. Those aren't His thoughts.

Those are our thoughts. In order to know God's thoughts, we need to look back at the Word. *"For My thoughts are not your thoughts, neither are your ways My ways,' declares the Lord."* (Isaiah 55:8)

There is no one else in this world more passionate about our families than God. If you're frustrated and agitated with family members right now, take heart. It's an opportunity to adjust your God Glasses and refocus your love.

Romans 8:31 (NKJ) says, *"...If God is for us, who can be against us?"* God isn't just referring to people who have a personal relationship with Him. He means everyone. He is *for* people. He loves you and He loves each member of your family: the good, the bad and, yes, the ugly. He wants your family to choose life and not death in your relationships so you can walk in all He has for you. He's pulling for all of you, all of the time.

You may have family members who refuse to let Jesus lead their lives. They may appear perfectly content to walk in the ways of the world. Do you know they are not disqualified from His being there for them? He loves them with an everlasting love.

Looking at them with your natural eyes, you probably feel a sense of hopelessness because all you can see are their circumstances, sometimes huge and overpowering. God wants you to see beyond their blindness. Put on your God Glasses so you can look into their hearts and you will be able to see them with the heart of God.

Keep your eyes on the prize and remember who you are, and whose you are. You may be the only example of God your family members see. Second Corinthians 2:14 says you are perfume to them! *"But thanks be to God, who always leads us in triumphal procession in Christ and through us spreads everywhere the fragrance of the knowledge of Him."* Walking in God's love and kindness attracts others to Jesus. God wants people to see Jesus in you. How you act affects their view of God. That's a pretty important responsibility, wouldn't you say?

Our little granddaughter, Allison, lives in another state so we don't see her as often as we would like. Everyday her mom and dad go through the family photo album and show her our pictures, pointing out Grandpa and Grandma. So even though Ally is just a toddler, she still recognizes us when we come for a visit. Although she hasn't had a close relationship with us in terms of proximity or spending lots of time with us, she knows and understands we are part of her family and that we love her very much. We aren't strangers to her because she knows what we look like and hears stories about us from her mom and dad. In many ways, it can be the same with you, your family, and Jesus. When your attitude and behavior reflect His nature to your family, they will see Him.

I love the fruit of the Spirit, don't you? Walking in love, joy, peace, patience, kindness, goodness, faithfulness, gentleness, self-control—and *grace* (not listed as a fruit of the Spirit, but clearly a very loving gift to give others!) allows your family to see Jesus in you. On the other hand, if you are being judgmental and unkind then that is the unfortunate impression they will have of Him, too.

It's so important to keep our God Glasses on so we can walk in love and not stumble. We need God's perspective so we can treat our families like He would. We need to be *like* God toward our families. Of course, I'm not saying that we can or should be "God" to them, but I am saying our lives should be full of godly qualities. We can hug our family members with God's loving arms. Sometimes that's not easy, especially when our flesh tempts us to act another way. With our God Glasses giving us His point of view, however, *all* things are possible. God wants His unconditional love to radiate through us to others.

We are given God's gift of love, not because of what we do, but because of who He is. We need to reach inside and draw on the power of the Holy Spirit to love others. As much as we genuinely love our families and want the best for them, God loves them far more than we are capable of and He passionately wants them to spend eternity with Him.

God gives each one of us an opportunity to accept Jesus, but it's up to us to make the choice. Second Peter 3:9 says, *"The Lord is not slow in keeping His promise, as some understand slowness. He is patient with you, not wanting anyone to perish, but everyone to come to repentance."* Such encouragement! God is pulling for our family members, yours and mine. He wants them to have the peace that comes from knowing Jesus as their best friend.

It's not always easy to love our families, in fact, sometimes it's easier to love someone else's family! God isn't condemning you, so you should not be condemning your family members. None of us are perfect. Luke 6:38 says, *"Give, and it will be given to you. A good measure, pressed down, shaken together..."* We know that Scripture with respect to our financial giving, but what about with respect to our spiritual giving to others? That would mean the same measure of judgment we give out can come back on us. Ouch! Who needs that? None of us need condemnation to weigh us down. When we generously give acceptance and unconditional love to our family, we can receive the same in return.

God never gave up on you and He won't give up on your family either. Whenever the temptation to throw in the towel on any of your family members comes, dig into Scripture, be encouraged, and wrap yourself in the Comforter who will cover you in the warmth of His love and restore you to the peace that surpasses all understanding.

Several years ago, I was in church praising the Lord and just loving Him, while at the same time, my heart was breaking for my children and some painful issues we were going through. In the middle of my praising, I sensed a deep, restful knowing in my heart as He spoke these words to me, "It's going to be okay with your children." In that moment the sorrow in my heart was replaced with overflowing joy. That is something only the Lord can do! The promise He made to me that day has never waned and my children are still doing fine.

God has promises for you concerning your family. You will find them in prayer, worship, and His Word. There you will hear Him speak those precious, magnificent promises to your heart, in accordance with His will. A word from the Lord is like an anchor to your soul, a lifeline of hope you can hang onto to when the winds of doubt begin to blow.

Have you ever had to wait for someone you love to hit bottom? Have you noticed that some people's "bottom" is far lower than what you would ever consider your own lowest of the low? Each of the gospels, Matthew, Mark, Luke, and John, relate the story of the prodigal son. While the son was out recklessly spending his inheritance on wild living, his father was grieved but did not interfere with his son's bad choices or try to rescue him from them. Instead, he patiently waited for his son to learn some very difficult life lessons.

Not until after the son had spent all of his money, was living in squalor, and eating what pigs wouldn't, did he finally come to the end of himself and realize there was no place like home. Only after he was allowed to feel the consequences of his actions was he able to humble himself and return to his family. There is no doubt in my mind that the long wait was nothing short of torture for his dad. And how did the father respond when he came back? Did he yell or sob through a very carefully prepared I-told-you-so lecture? No! He threw him a party!

Like many of us would be inclined to do, the father could have sat his son down and sternly pointed out each and every one of his son's mistakes, showing him the error of his ways so he would never, *ever* put his father threw that kind of torment *again*! But he didn't choose to do that. Instead, he chose to love him because he was his son. The father knew his son had just learned many valuable yet very difficult lessons—the hard way. He accepted him with loving arms, just as your heavenly Father accepts you.

Your own earthly father may not have been able to show love to you this way. Be careful not to attribute your earthly father's flaws and limitations to your heavenly Father. It's not fair to either of them. Even if you had the world's greatest dad, the most loving, generous, faithful father, his love would still pale in comparison to the love of Father God, who can and does love you unconditionally. His more-than-enough love is yours. Spend time with Him and share His love with your family. As you do, they will hear Him gently, lovingly say, "Come home. All is forgiven."

People need second chances, an opportunity to start over. Thankfully we serve the God of Second Chances. The thief hanging on a cross next to Jesus at Golgotha knew his own sin and why he was on his cross. At the moment he was at death's door, he recognized Jesus and knew that He was being unjustly crucified. The thief looked into the eyes of His Savior, who saw his heart and his sorrow. With the compassion and forgiveness that can only come from the Messiah, Jesus said to him, "...*Today you will be with Me in paradise.*"

Frankly, we would all like to see our family members walking with God *yesterday* so we can stop holding our proverbial breath, and exhale. But with God, it doesn't matter how late it is in life when someone comes to Him. If a person still has breath in their body, there is still time to get right with God. He knows the beginning and the end. He is not affected by the clock or the calendar. We are.

Sometimes we just need to back off, give people space, and not be judgmental. It's really not our God-given assignment to be looking over anyone's shoulder to make sure they're getting it right. Trying to be the Holy Spirit in someone else's life can wear you out. Instead, we need to just turn them over to God, saying, "Lord, I place them in Your hands. It's the safest place for them to be." We can't control or change people, and truthfully, God doesn't want us to try. It's not our job. Our job is to give them God's unconditional love out of a pure heart, in spite of what our loved ones are saying or doing. He loves us right where we are and wants us to do the same for others.

The Bible tells us it is the goodness of God that leads men to repentance. Knowing God's mercy, love, and forgiveness causes us to say, "Oh Lord, I am so sorry! You are so good to me. I don't deserve You!" When our hearts are open to God, it's easier to repent and receive His love.

I've heard it said, "Words are like containers. They carry things from one place to another." If that is true, our words can carry things to our family members: love and blessings or guilt and condemnation. In Proverbs 10:19 (NKJ), it says, *"In the multitude of words sin is not lacking, but he who restrains his lips is wise."* Sometimes what we *don't* say is more important than what we *do* say. We may have the right intention in our hearts but somehow the craziest things can come flying out of our mouths when we least expect it. Unfortunately words can't be reeled back in once they're spoken. Occasionally we will be granted a "do over" but it's better to choose our words carefully from the get-go because they form our environment. Proverbs 14:1 says, *"The wise woman builds her house, but with her own hands the foolish one tears hers down."* If we are careful and purposeful with our words, we will like the house we build. If we are careless and reckless with our words, we may find ourselves living in a house where we really don't want to live! Speak encouraging words to your family.

Sometimes when I'm meditating on the Word of God, mental images about a passage appear like word pictures. I was thinking about Psalm 141:3 (NKJ), *"Set a guard, O Lord, over my mouth; keep a watch over the door of my lips."* As I was thinking about it, I saw a steel gate over my mouth, the kind you see in movies when the enemy is approaching the castle entrance and just in the nick of time the gate slams shut before the enemy can enter. That is what needs to happen with our mouths sometimes. We need to listen to the Lord and before we allow hurtful words to come charging through, we need to close the doors of our lips!

I would love to tell you that I've always been successful in this area, but really I haven't. Sometimes hurtful words escape my mouth, then I fall on my knees before the Lord and tell Him, "I blew it again. I can't do this without You, Lord. I didn't mean to say the things I said. Forgive me. I blew it again." And, you know what? His mercies are new *every* morning and He is faithful to forgive me and help me again and again. He'll enable you through His strength too.

The truth is none of us are perfect. As much as we would like to believe otherwise, we are not perfect parents and we are not perfect spouses. The good news is God isn't asking us to be perfect. He just asks us to trust Him. Then He can help us relate to others with His perfect love.

When I accepted the Lord over thirty years ago, He filled me with so much love I couldn't contain it. I had great zeal but, quite honestly, my tactics in sharing His love might have been lacking a little wisdom. I somehow (quite erroneously, I might add) thought I should let my family members know the truth and the right way to believe. I had been raised in a particular denomination where things were done in a liturgical, rather strict way. I thought I should let everyone know they were wrong and I was right. My tactics were a little rough. God saw my heart and did use me, but not everyone was open and receptive to my message because of the way I shared it. After all, how right are you when you tell everyone else they are wrong?

When I received God's love, it totally swept me off my feet. I was so head over heels in love with Jesus, it consumed me. Unfortunately, those around me were not as excited as I was about my newly discovered love. If I was to be the fragrance of Christ, I may have doused myself a little too strongly. You know what it's like when someone walks into the room wearing too much perfume. Everyone scatters. Today I know better, but my zeal back then was pushing people away from God, rather than drawing them closer.

Jesus is irresistible. There's no doubt. He said in John 12:32 (NKJ), *"And I, if I am lifted up from the earth, will draw all peoples to Myself."* Rightly spoken words can attract people to Jesus. Misused words can alienate them. Choose your words wisely. We all make mistakes, but thankfully God looks at our hearts and knows when we're trying our best. Stay sensitive to Him and be open to His correction. Pray for your family members and trust God to take care of the rest. In Matthew 9:37-38, Jesus tells His disciples to pray for people to be sent to share the Good News with those who don't know Him yet.

You can pray and ask the Lord to send the right people into your family member's lives. It may not be you who they can hear the truth from. Even Jesus wasn't accepted in His own hometown. Some of the people in His early life who were His friends and family couldn't see Jesus for who He really was. It may be like that with your family too, so ask God to send someone your family will listen to. Galatians 6:7 says, *"...A man reaps what he sows."* We all have family who need to hear about the goodness of God. Instead of you trying to tell them again, go and share the Good News with someone else's family and trust God to send someone to share it with yours. In the meantime, continue using your God Glasses.

God is always faithful to His Word and will take us where He wants us to be. Deuteronomy 29:29 (NCV) says, *"There are some things the Lord our God has kept secret, but there are some things He has let us know. These things belong to us and our children forever so that we will do everything in these teachings."* Pray for your family members and trust God for the best.

Please don't put your God Glasses away. The longer you keep them hidden in a drawer, the harder it is to find them and put them back where they belong. Don't let your God Glasses slip from your nose!

PEOPLE NEED LOVE, ESPECIALLY WHEN THEY DON'T DESERVE IT.

–UNKNOWN

six

seeing your finances as
GOD SEES THEM

Have you noticed a correlation between your level of peace and where you are at with your financial situation? You don't have to be swimming in dough to have peace, but as long as you can pay your bills and have a bit left over, you can experience a comfortable level of peace. So, what happens when, out of the clear blue sky, you are suddenly hit with an unexpected financial bomb? *Wham!* Suddenly, peace flies out the window and stress charges in like a bull in a china shop!

No financial bombs surprise the Lord. In fact, His Word actually warns us that in this world we will have trials, tribulation, distress and frustration. (See John 16:33 AMP.) We live in this world, so we might as well get used to the fact that trouble will come, even in our finances. Be encouraged! God knew it all beforehand and has a plan to help us through whatever challenges come our way. As we lean on Him for direction, He will bless us in the midst of our trials.

First Peter 1:23 says the Word of God is an incorruptible seed. God put the principle of sowing and reaping in place from the beginning, for our blessing. Look at Genesis 8:22: *"As long as the earth endures, seedtime and harvest, cold and heat, summer and winter, day and night will never cease."* Seedtime and harvest are part of the Lord's plan. Adam and Eve knew this principle well. They understood the process of planting seeds and collecting crops. Today, unless we farm for a living or have a vegetable garden in the summer, we don't typically think in these terms.

God gave us His seed principle so we could understand how His kingdom works. The principle of sowing and reaping is not only true in the spiritual realm, but also in the natural one. It applies to all areas of our lives. In the context of this chapter, we will discuss how it applies to our finances. It's important for us to see our finances as God sees them. We can do this by putting on our God Glasses.

If you plant tomato seeds then you will reap tomatoes. If you bless God's kingdom through your giving, you will also reap blessings in your life as well as storing up treasure in heaven. The incorruptible seed of God's Word produces blessing every time. When we act in faith, we can be convinced His promises will come to pass in our lives.

In the parable of the Sower, God shows us the seed is the Word of God and the soil is our hearts. If we were to simply toss a packet of good tomato seeds into the garden, some of those seeds might grow but the likelihood of a full harvest is slim since we didn't follow the planting instructions properly. If we follow the planting directions and the seed is good but the soil has rocks and weeds, producing a full harvest will remain questionable. The seed of God's Word, however, will produce a guaranteed harvest, without fail. Just as natural seed needs favorable conditions to grow, so God needs our cooperation.

In Luke 6:38 (NKJ), we learn more about the principle of sowing and reaping: *"Give, and it will be given to you: good measure, pressed down, shaken together, and running over will be put into your bosom. For with the same measure that you use, it will be measured back to you."* This is a promise. Whatever you sow, you are going to reap; whatever you give to others, you will also receive.

God wants us to have an attitude, a heart, for giving. He promises that as we give, it will be given back to us. We know God is the One who causes us to increase because Deuteronomy 8:18 says God gives us the power to get wealth. It is God's plan and His intention to fulfill all our needs. Some people believe this principle. They know it is a spiritual law. "Give" and you will "get." But God sees our hearts, too. He knows when we are giving only so we will get. That's the wrong motive. Giving out of love is the right motive. God demonstrated His love for us by giving us His Son. When we give out of love for others, it allows God to complete that spiritual law and give back to us.

The more we develop our relationship with God, the better we will be at discerning His voice in regards to our giving *and* receiving. He wants us to be willing to sow whenever and wherever He leads us. As such, it's important to learn to discern, or recognize, when we are being led by the Spirit and when we are being manipulated by someone else or by our own motives.

When God wants to bless someone, in nearly every situation He uses His people to carry out His purposes. God likes to use people, just like you and me, to meet the needs of others. Seriously, if money grew on trees, what would be the point? Once you've tasted what it's like to give to God, His way, it can almost be addictive. Giving is so much fun and a great blessing! Now who wouldn't want to be a part of that plan? But here's the deal: You have to be led by His Spirit and not led by your own thoughts or feelings.

Let me tell you about what happened to me in my self-determination and (Oh, how I dislike admitting this!) lack of discernment. Several years ago, I was having a garage sale and had a beautiful comforter for sale, prominently displayed for all to see. Many people admired it and wanted to buy it but a man grabbed it and told me he really wanted to buy it. Then he told me he would have to go home and get the money. He was about to put the comforter down when I, wanting to be the "model" Christian demonstrating godly goodness (and so he would think I was wonderful) told him he could take it home and just bring back the money.

You already know how this ended, right? The guy made off with my beautiful comforter and I never saw him again. That wasn't Spirit-led giving. It was *prideful* giving! I learned a lesson in how *not* to be led by the "spirit." I quickly realized I hadn't been led by God's Spirit at all. I had been led by my own motives. The moral of the story? Keep your God Glasses on and be led by *His* Spirit!

A few years back when my husband, Ray, and I were at a conference, I saw a couple I felt in my spirit needed money and

I asked Ray if it was okay to give them some. I'm blessed to be married to a particularly generous, giving man. That helps make giving easy and fun for me. Sometimes though, a willingness to give frequently can ignore God's purpose and plan—the story of the comforter, above, is a fine example—so learning life's lessons has caused me to double check my motives.

I looked at that couple and thought, "Surely, everyone can tell they need money." That made me wonder whether this was about to be Linda-led giving or Jesus-led giving. I could see they needed the money, or at least I thought they did. They *looked* like they needed it, didn't they? I found myself asking, "Lord, is this you?" When you give money to perfect strangers, you want to be sure it's God and that the assignment is yours!

I checked with Ray again, wanting to see if I was seeing correctly. "Ray," I said, "*You* can tell they need money, can't you?" He said, "No, but if you feel led to give them money, go ahead and do it." It was so real to me. I thought everyone could see it but that just wasn't the case. To me it was obvious they were in need, not because of what they were wearing, but because of something I saw with my God Glasses. The Lord was revealing it to *me*. That day I knew I was being led by His Spirit, so I obeyed Him and gave. I share these two instances of giving to show how wrong I was in one situation but how right I was in another. I learned a great lesson! Listening with your heart and being led by His Spirit are paramount.

Ephesians 4:28 (AMP) says, *"Let the thief steal no more, but rather let him be industrious, making an honest living with his own hands, so that he may be able to give to those in need."* God's ultimate purpose isn't simply for us to gain wealth so we become rich and go on lots of vacations. His plan is so much bigger than that. (That being said, please understand God is also not *against* us enjoying ourselves either.) His ultimate purpose is for our financial increase to further the kingdom. God gives you the power to get wealth so you have seed to eat and seed to sow. He always wants us to be looking ahead and asking ourselves, "How can I help? Lord, where can I plant seed for Your kingdom and Your honor?"

Ray and I have a little saying between the two of us. "If God can get it through you, He will get it to you." It's true! God will bless you so you can bless others. The truth is you can never out-give God. Now you may ask, "How do we get the seed to give?" Okay, brace yourself. Are you ready? Get a job and work! I love the biblical story of the tax money found in the mouth of a fish as much as the next person (See Matthew 17:27.) but I mean, really, how many mornings have you opened your eyes to a bed covered in money? (If you have such an experience, I'll want to interview you for my next book!) Although He certainly can, it's unusual for the Lord to provide money to us in those ways. He usually provides for us through the work of our hands. Even if our job isn't a high paying one, we will still have seed we can sow. It may be a small amount, but it can yield big returns when you obey His leading. Sowing seeds of diligence and faithfulness on the job can also lead to promotion or a better job.

He takes us step by step in the perfect plan He has for us. Obey His voice and follow Him. If we are faithful with a little, He will make us ruler over much. That is one of His promises to us.

Perhaps your current job isn't your dream job. Be faithful where you have been planted and you will be on your way to a better place, but watch the words of your mouth. Words are seed. Kind and faith-filled words are good seed and produce a good crop. Grumbling and complaining words are bad seed and produce a bad crop. It's a pretty simple concept really, isn't it?

When Ray and I moved to California in 1994, relocating was a blessing. Ray had been hired by a particular company and shortly after, the same company hired me. Ray visited job sites and I assisted the office secretary. Prior to moving from Missouri to California, I had only worked part-time. In California, our hours were *l-o-n-g*. I wasn't used to those kinds of hours and found it pretty difficult. I whined and complained a lot, but by doing so I wasn't showing how grateful I was for the opportunity God had given us.

Each day we would arrive at work at 7 a.m. and usually didn't leave until after 7 at night. Never having worked full-time before, I had been rather sheltered from the not-so-nice-people-of-the-world and wasn't used to being around folks like that, especially for twelve hours plus a day! I was asked to "Do this. Do that. Pick this up. And, pick that up." It was tough physically, mentally, spiritually and emotionally. There I was, surrounded. Exhausted. And too tired to put on my God Glasses.

By the end of most days, I just wanted to go home and have a good cry. Sometimes I did. In my heart, I would say, "God, I want to be grateful for this job. Please help me." I began looking at the good things: I was there with my husband; money was coming in regularly. In a very short time, my God Glasses were securely in place and my view of the situation completely changed! My vision, not the situation, was different. What we see with our spiritual eyes, in accordance with God's truth, is the true reality of our natural circumstances. It's all about perspective.

The Lord is so faithful. He eventually moved Ray and me from where we were to the new place He wanted us to be—a better, more prosperous place. By His grace, He showed us what to do there. We had the ability to see clearly and follow His leading because we both made sure we were wearing our God Glasses every day.

The real point of this story is about what *didn't* happen. I didn't stay where I was. I could have if I continued whining, grumbling, and complaining to everyone. I believe wherever we are, we can be faithful to and grateful for what God has given us. Circumstances aren't always up to us but our attitudes definitely are. As the saying goes, "Attitude isn't just anything. It's everything!"

When we find ourselves in uncomfortable circumstances that were never part of our own plan, we can always find things for which we can be grateful. Thankfulness offered with a sincere, obedient heart will change your perspective and your circumstances. We are not to be grateful so that our circumstances will change. We are to be grateful because they *can* change.

God's plan is so much bigger than ours! With each step of faith, He lights our path. He doesn't illuminate the entire journey. If He did, we wouldn't need to rely on Him. He wants us to trust Him through everything. We don't always understand what role we're playing in God's kingdom, but in 1 Corinthians 3:6-7 (NKJ), Paul tells us, *"I planted, Apollos watered, but God gave the increase.*

So then neither he who plants is anything, nor he who waters, but God who gives the increase." The person who plants and the person who waters are on the same team. Each will receive a reward according to his or her own labor. We are called to work together because we are all a part of what God is doing. Whatever part you play in your own life or someone else's, be obedient to God. Your obedience is like water, sunshine, and fertilizer on God's incorruptible seed, allowing it to grow and become ripe for harvest.

There is another seed example I would like to share with you. Some time ago, Ray and I were standing in the check-out lane at Wal-Mart when I noticed an elderly woman in front of us. She was preparing to pay for her groceries but was fumbling in her purse for her money. I knew instantly in my spirit she had to count every penny she had. I whispered to Ray that I wanted to pay for her groceries, and of course he agreed, so I quietly told the cashier. Her surprised reply was, *"Really?* Are you going to let her know?" I hadn't thought that far but realized I would certainly need to tell her. When I did, her eyes filled with tears as she looked at us both in disbelief. "No one has ever done anything like this for me before," she said. I looked her in the eyes and said, "We just want you to know how much God loves you." This time the tears started streaming down her face. "No one has *ever* done that before," she repeated.

Who do you think was blessed? Certainly the woman receiving the paid groceries was blessed, but Ray and I were extremely blessed, too. What a privilege to be used by God in His plan to help that precious woman. We weren't the only part of God's plan for her but we were the Walmart-grocery-payment part. We did what God told us, and He used it to demonstrate His over-the-top-beyond-comprehension abundant love to an elderly woman on a sunny afternoon. Now, that's my idea of getting in on the action!

I encourage you to be sensitive to the Lord's leading. When you wear your God Glasses, you will see more opportunities to give. Don't undervalue what you have to offer. Sometimes when you hand someone a gift for no apparent reason and for no special occasion, they will look at you in shock. Probably no one has ever given them something "just because." Maybe they have never been told they are loved and valuable to God. You never know how your giving can bless someone's life until it happens. Give what you have and God will take care of the rest.

My friend and her son were at a gas station and saw a homeless man digging through the trash for aluminum cans. She only had a couple dollars with her but gave what she had to the man and drove away. Her son said, "Mom, I wish we could have done more." She looked at him, saw his tender heart toward the man and said, "Well then, let's go to the bank!" She wasn't wealthy but she went to an ATM and withdrew twenty dollars. They went back and found the man going through another trash can and handed him the money. To this day they don't know the entire picture of how their kindness affected that homeless man's life, but God does. What's important is they were led by God's Spirit and obeyed. If God is prompting you to do something, do it, and then watch your life change for the better.

Philippians 4:15-18 (NKJ) says, "*Now you Philippians know also that in the beginning of the gospel, when I departed from Macedonia, no church shared with me concerning giving and receiving but you only. For even in Thessalonica you sent aid once and again for my necessities. Not that I seek the gift, but I seek the fruit that abounds on your account. Indeed I have all and abound. I am full, having received from Epaphroditus the things sent from you, a sweet-smelling aroma, an acceptable sacrifice, well pleasing to God."*

That verse is so good! Paul is saying to the Philippian church, "Thank you for giving to me. I am so grateful for everything you have done. When no one else would, you gave to me." He added, "It's not that I need the gift. I don't need your money." He goes on to say, "I've learned to live with a lot, and I have learned to live with little, but what I want is for you to give so that fruit can abound in your giving." Paul knew the secret. He knew giving causes increase in the life of the giver.

As I said earlier, if we give only so we can get, our hearts are not in the right place. God always looks at the heart. Your eyes need to be on Jesus and the opportunities He puts in your path.

"...He who sows sparingly will also reap sparingly, and he who sows bountifully will also reap bountifully. So let each one give as he purposes in his heart, not grudgingly or out of necessity; for God loves a cheerful giver. And God is able to make all grace abound toward you, that you, always having all sufficiency in all things, may have abundance for every good work." (2 Corinthians 9:6-8 NKJ) When you take your eyes off of your own need and ask God how you can be used to meet the needs of another, blessings will come into your life. Will you be a cheerful giver in someone's life today? Don't take those God Glasses off.

FAITH MEANS TRUSTING IN ADVANCE WHAT WILL ONLY MAKE SENSE IN REVERSE.

–PHILIP YANCEY

seven

seeing your situation
AS GOD SEES IT

A re you standing at the foot of a huge, seemingly insurmountable mountain-of-a-problem in your life? Are you convinced that mountain is impossible to conquer because you can't find a way around it, and you haven't found a way through it? As it looms ominously before you, are you feeling helpless and hopeless, just wanting to give up?

Focusing on the overwhelming size of the problem can at best blind you and at worst paralyze you. You are feeling this way because you are trying to solve the problem in your own strength. Quit trying to figure things out! God is inviting you to trust Him in your circumstance. So, put on your God Glasses. A new perspective awaits you.

Often we see the situations in our lives and the problems we face differently than God does. We may be looking through distorted glasses that make challenges seem impossible, and sometimes even hopeless. If we can look beyond our natural eyes and see through God's Word, we will see our situation from God's perspective.

Matthew 19:26 assures us that what is impossible with man is possible with God. Did you notice those two words right there? With Him. All things are possible *with* Him. This is so important for us to understand, it's repeated four times in the gospels! Give your mountain to God. Relax. Take a deep breath and put your trust in the One who moves mountains. It's His business! He is completely worthy of your trust and able to do exceedingly, abundantly, above and beyond all you could ever ask or think.

We always like to try to figure everything out, don't we? Don't waste time calculating the next fourteen steps you think you need to take to solve the problem yourself. There is an answer, but you won't find it in your head. When you believe He is able to do what He says He will, your faith pleases God. Just take it one step at a time, starting with the first step God shows you. He can lead you around, through, or over your mountain—and occasionally, He might just move it out of your way. When you choose to rely on Him, you won't be disappointed because God is the Good Shepherd who takes good care of His sheep.

The Word of God is a lamp to your feet and a light to your path. (See Psalm 119:105.) You may not always know how He's going to bring you through a situation, but He will bring you through. God likes it when you rely on Him. Usually He doesn't fully reveal the entire roadmap all at once but He does provide flawless direction, lighting each step of the way so you can see where your feet are about to go to avoid falling in a ditch or stubbing your toe on a rock. He will show you what you need to see, even when your surroundings seem dark and unclear.

Your God Glasses will provide a focused view of your next step. By continually following God's guidance, you will stay on the right path.

I certainly have not lived a problem-free life. No one has. Still, I can encourage you to trust God with your problems because of what I have experienced with the Lord, who has proven Himself to be true to me again and again. He will be true to you, too!

There have been nights I've gone to bed feeling crushed by the weight of an impossible problem, only to wake up the next morning to His perfect solution for me. His Word directs my path even while I'm sleeping. Wow. Think of it. You can be on the brink of despair one night but experience joy and peace in the morning. We may not be able to change our circumstances immediately, but we are can trust the One who can.

Blowing up a balloon to just short of the breaking point illustrates the way we can feel when pressures continue to build and build. Pressure can take us to the point of explosion. Are you facing a problem so overwhelming that you think you can't take it any longer? Giving up may sound like a solution, but it is not God's solution. The God of the Breakthrough has a plan for every breakdown. We don't always know how close we are to breakthrough in the situation, but Gods does. He has your answer. Rather than hanging in there with white knuckle endurance, hang on to Him.

King David poured out his heart writing psalms to the Lord. He wrote, *"Now David was greatly distressed, for the people spoke of stoning him, because the soul of all the people was grieved, every man for his sons and for his daughters. But David strengthened himself in the Lord His God."* (1 Samuel 30:6 NKJ) David built himself up in the Lord by spending time thinking about Him. When things became hard for him, he would write another song to the Lord. He knew where his answers came from and that God was on his side. David had his own special pair of God Glasses.

You can look at your situation as a glass half-full or a glass half-empty. People with a negative outlook will say, "It's too hard. My situation will never change." But people with a positive outlook will say, "Things are going to get better. It's just a matter of time. God is with me and I'm relying on Him." The choice is yours. You can see your circumstance as a problem or as an opportunity to have an adventure with God.

Years before Ray and I moved to California, we were in a very difficult financial place in our lives. We owned a business that was going downhill fast but we chose to trust and obey God through those tough times. We gave when He told us to give, forgave when He told us to forgive, and showed others love even when we didn't feel like it. We were confronted with many seemingly impossible obstacles to overcome but the Lord always showed us the next step. Eventually we were given an opportunity to move to California where we now live. Never in our wildest dreams or our best-laid plans did we think the Lord would move these two Midwesterners to California as an answer to our prayers. But He did. When we arrived in California, we didn't have much left to call our own, but just as He promised in His Word, God refreshed us in the desert and made a way when there seemed to be no way.

Because of the sheer magnitude of restoration work needed after the Northridge earthquake of 1994, our employer had to hire many people, including us. We were provided with a place to live, a company car, and a cell phone—all paid for by our employer. We were even given a food allowance! We really didn't think life could get any better, especially considering everything we had lost.

At one point, we had a little time to ourselves so we decided to drive to San Diego. We could not really do much in our free time because we just didn't have much money to spend, but we did have a car. We had received an invitation from a time-share company, so out of curiosity we stopped at their office on our way to San Diego and watched a presentation about property on Coronado Island. In exchange for our time, we received a free dinner for two at the famous Coronado Hotel, a tour of the island, and a private visit to see the property. We were so *blessed*! At the end of the day, we had spent a grand total of seven dollars because we splurged for an ice cream on the way home. It was a beautiful day and we really enjoyed each other's company. What had seemed impossible to us was not impossible with God. He made a way for us to have a lovely day together.

Ray and I have learned to depend on the Lord's faithfulness and not on the situations of our lives. It's a great way to live and it pleases our Father. Wearing our God Glasses gives us the ability to look beyond what we see with our natural eyes to what God always sees. Our natural eyes provide us with limited vision, but when we put on our God Glasses we can see beyond to see what He sees.

One of my favorite Old Testament stories paints a clear picture of how God sees. It talks about real God Glasses. Well, they aren't really called God Glasses in the Bible, but if you read

2 Kings 6 you will see what I mean. In the city where the prophet Elisha was, the Syrian king was frustrated because everywhere his army went to fight against the king of Israel, the Israelites knew his army was coming. The king was getting very tired of this and thought someone was spying on him in his bedroom. One of his servants told him the prophet, Elisha, knew what was going on in his bedroom because he heard from God. The king of Syria then decided if this Elisha fellow was the problem, he was going to have to capture him.

That night after Elisha and his servant went to bed, the Syrian army surrounded the city. His servant heard a noise, got up to see what it was, and found the entire Syrian army outside! Very much afraid, he woke Elisha and told him what he had seen.

By faith, Elisha told his servant there were more warriors out there who were *for* them than against them! The servant looked again and still didn't see it that way. (He probably should have reached for his God Glasses!) Elisha prayed God would help his servant see beyond his natural eyes so he could see the army of God. When his servant was suddenly able to see the truth of the situation—the mountain was actually covered with angels and chariots of fire—he wasn't afraid anymore! Imagine that!

Isn't that an awesome faith-building story? It demonstrates how limited we are when we only see with our natural eyes, but if we put on our God Glasses we can see God's truth.

Perhaps you can't see beyond your current situation and it appears there is a mighty army ready to overtake you. Ask God to show you what you need to see in order to face your situation. Just as He opened the spiritual eyes of Elisha's servant to see what his natural eyes could not, God can open your eyes too. He will show you He's working on your behalf.

God desires to see your dreams become reality. When you enjoy hanging out with Jesus, you can be sure your dreams and desires were deposited in your heart by Him. How do I know that? Because His Word tells me! Psalm 37:4 says, *"Delight yourself in the Lord and He will give you the desires of your heart."*

God doesn't want us to rely on our natural vision alone to determine the truth. What we see isn't always what we get. That's why we need to look through our God Glasses. I learned this more clearly shortly after we moved to California.

One evening around sunset, I was on my way home from work and drove by a man standing in front of his car with the hood up. Normally I count on my husband to assist stranded men on the side of the road, but this time I noticed the familiar Christian fish symbol on the bumper of his car and instantly saw a connection with him as my brother in Christ. "He is a stranger, yes, but we Christians need to stick together!" I thought. So I drove around the block praying for the right thing to say and do.

Pulling up next to his car, I rolled down my window and said, "Sir, do you need help?" "Yes," he said, "my car won't start." He told me he lived nearby and asked if I would give him a ride. My mind raced. "I'm a woman driving alone at night and I'm about to give a stranger—a man—a ride. But hey, he's a Christian," I reasoned. I only hesitated for a second, and then said, "Sure! Get in."

We drove to his apartment, mostly in silence. Finally I just had to ask. "Aren't you surprised a woman driving alone would not only stop to help you, but also give you a ride this late at night?

He looked puzzled, so I explained, "I saw the fish symbol on your car so I knew you were a Christian and wanted to help you!" I was so excited to share that with him! "Oh, that…" he said dryly, "That was on my car when I bought it." I couldn't believe it. Guess I forgot to wear my God Glasses that day!

Why don't we keep our God Glasses on? What keeps us from choosing to see beyond the natural into what God sees? Many times it's fear. God has great things in store for you, but if you put more faith in your fear than in the faithfulness of God, it may be difficult to put your trust in Him in order to receive from Him. If you struggle with the fear of failure, ask God to strengthen your inner man. Spend time studying His Word and praying to build your faith on the truth.

Don't focus on gloom and doom news stories you see on television or read in the newspaper. Whatever you give your attention to will affect your thinking. Romans 12:2 tells us not to be conformed to this world but be transformed by renewing your mind. In other words, let God's Word change your mind. He will help you if you ask Him. Be tenacious. Just because there hasn't been success in your past doesn't mean there won't be success in your future. Be prepared to hold on and hang on. Your old ways of thinking didn't happen overnight. Breaking those habits will take determination. Dwelling on failure won't bring success either, but dwelling on success is sure to move you away from failure! You can shift from having a fear of failure to being excited about what God can and will do for you.

Comparing your life to someone else's is a trick from the enemy. Getting caught in the I-want-to-be-like-them or the I-want-to-have-what-they-have trap will keep you from receiving all God has for *you*. Don't compare yourself to anyone else. God has a plan and purpose for *your* life. Keep your focus there and move in that direction. You are who God made you to be. You have special talents, abilities, and gifting He gave only to you. Stay on *your* course and be the best *you* can be. If you've given up, get back up! It is not over! You have another chance with the God of Second Chances. It will take putting your God Glasses on and keeping them on, even if things begin to feel a little scary.

Now I'd like us to look at an awesome Scripture, one that would be good for you to memorize. *"Now to Him who is able to do exceedingly abundantly above all that we ask or think, according to the power that works in us, to Him be glory in the church by Christ Jesus to all generations, forever and ever."* (Ephesians 3:20-21 NKJ) The power of the Holy Spirit is available to you. You just have to tap into it.

Faith is not some magic wand we use to get God to move on our behalf and cause things to happen. The fact is, God has *already* moved and it's *already* happened. By faith, we just have to take hold of what He has provided. The Bible says the Word of God is eternal. It's everlasting. God said heaven and earth will pass away but His Word will never pass away.

Allow God to paint the canvas of your mind with the beautiful picture He has for your life. You will find it in His Word.

YOU ARE
GIVEN
A SITUATION.
WHAT
YOU ARE
DETERMINES
WHAT YOU
SEE; WHAT
YOU SEE
DETERMINES
WHAT YOU
DO.

–HADDON ROBINSON

eight

seeing your enemies as
GOD SEES THEM

8

I love to study God's Word. That alone is proof that I'm a new creation in Christ because during high school, studying certainly wasn't on my top-ten list of things to do! But when I gave my heart to the Lord, He came in and revamped everything about me, teaching me His ways and changing me for His good. Now, studying His Word is my constant delight and I continue to grow in every way as a result. Through His Word, I can see the truth with my spiritual eyes wide open. I can see people and situations the way God sees them because I'm wearing my God Glasses. Knowing the truth makes it easy to recognize the voice behind the lies that Satan tries to whisper in my ear. Studying the truth exercises and strengthens my God-given gift of discernment. The same is true for you.

The devil is a liar. It's his job and he takes it seriously. Jesus called him the father of lies in John 8:44. The very essence of murderous hatred, Satan loathes God and all of mankind. He works tirelessly to convince each of us that people are the source of conflict in our lives. That is pure deception. We must remember the devil's native language is the language of lies and we are his target. His mission is to destroy. Constantly working to convince us his ways are right and God's ways are wrong, the devil uses people, and yes, (gulp!) sometimes he even uses you and me to hurt others. Well, there you have it. We are imperfect beings, but that doesn't mean we have free reign to willfully participate in Satan's plans to do harm to anyone.

Shortly after I was born again, I unintentionally offended someone because of my lack of maturity and understanding of God's ways. I spoke some things I genuinely wished I hadn't. I apologized when I realized what I had done wrong and admitted what I had said had been foolish. Nonetheless, it was a real cause for offense and I felt absolutely terrible about it. I had not only offended a dear woman, but also her best friend. Afterwards, whenever I saw either of them, I would avoid eye contact so I wouldn't be reminded of my appalling blunder. I carried a heavy burden of guilt and shame because of what I had done.

Many years later, I had an opportunity to have lunch with that same woman. As the time drew closer, a sense of dread came over me. I recalled my "big bad blunder" made so many years earlier. It still weighed heavily on me and I was embarrassed just thinking about it. Yuck! Have you ever been there?

Nevertheless, I gathered my courage and went to the lunch, in spite of the dread I was feeling. Thankfully we enjoyed our time together from the moment we were seated, chatting aimlessly about many topics. But no matter how hard I tried not to, I kept seeing that great big pink elephant sitting there between us. Finally I just couldn't take it anymore and blurted, "I have to talk to you about something!" She looked surprised, but graciously listened as I bared my soul, recalling the incident when I offended her and her friend so many years earlier and apologizing once again for the foolish things I had said. With genuine concern she stopped me saying, "Linda, I don't know what you're talking about." Stunned, I looked at her. "Don't you remember way back then?" I asked. "No, I really don't," she said. I couldn't believe it. She didn't even have memory of what had happened! The huge pink elephant I thought was between us all those years didn't even exist!

I learned an important lesson that day. Condemnation, lies, and guilt come from the enemy of our souls and his tactics are meant to destroy our relationships. Like bricks and mortar, he piles lies cemented with guilt, condemnation, and unforgiveness until his dividing wall completely separates us from people and from God. Just as darkness has to leave when light enters a room, so the enemy's wall crumbles when we put on our God Glasses and God's truth about a situation is revealed.

When we get angry with someone, the enemy is more than happy to help us lash out in retaliation. The moment an offense takes place, one of Satan's cohort's comes flying onto our shoulder and begins feeding lies into our ear. We can choose to agree with the enemy, allowing his words to fester and grow in our hearts, or we can peacefully put on our God Glasses, call out to God, and receive His truth and encouragement in the midst of what would have otherwise been an ugly situation.

Let's look at Ephesians 6:12 (NKJ). *"For we do not wrestle against flesh and blood, but against principalities, against powers, against the rulers of the darkness of this age, against spiritual hosts of wickedness in the heavenly places."*

Our true enemy is Satan, the ruler of darkness, principalities and powers. He doesn't play fairly. Satan can use people to wreak havoc in other peoples' lives when they are willing to give in to his tactics. But, when we know who the real enemy is many battles fought in the natural realm can be avoided. We put on our God Glasses so we can stand against everything the devil throws our way. The more we know Jesus, who defeated our enemy when He rose from the dead, and the more we know the power He placed inside of us, the easier it is to stand and do the right thing.

In Matthew 16:21-23 (NKJ), Jesus tells His disciples what He was about to go through, including His own death and resurrection. *"From that time Jesus began to show to His disciples that He must go to Jerusalem, and suffer many things from the elders and chief priests and scribes, and be killed, and be raised the third day. Then Peter took Him aside and began to rebuke Him, saying, 'Far be it from You, Lord; this shall not happen to You!' But He turned and said to Peter, 'Get behind Me, Satan! You are an offense to Me, for you are not mindful of the things of God, but the things of men.'"*

We can certainly empathize with Peter in that moment, can't we? We would not have wanted to accept what Jesus was saying either. This was *not* good news! My guess is, Peter may have stopped listening the moment Jesus said He was going to suffer and die. Our limited minds can only take so much! He may not have heard the words "and raised on the third day." Instead, focusing on the "suffer and die" part, his heart broke. He didn't want to think about Jesus not being there with him anymore, let alone that He would have to suffer.

Like so many of us would have done in that moment, Peter responded by taking Jesus aside and arguing, "Never, Lord! This shall never happen to you!" But Jesus looked at Peter and said, "Get behind me, Satan! You are a stumbling block to Me." Although Peter's intentions were his own and not God's, Jesus was not saying, "Peter you are the devil." Jesus was showing Peter that he was agreeing with the devil by trying to prevent Him from fulfilling His purpose.

Jesus was not about to be diverted from His God-ordained mission here on earth. He was not angry with Peter. He understood the frame of mind he was in and the emotions behind his statement. Nevertheless, Jesus knew His purpose and fulfilled it, head on.

By His example, Jesus demonstrated the truth of Ephesians 6:12 for us by directly addressing the tempter, and not Peter, separating the person from the voice of the ruler of darkness who was actually speaking. We need to learn from Jesus' example so we will operate in the same way.

First Peter 5:8 says, *Be self-controlled and alert. Your enemy the devil prowls around like a roaring lion looking for someone to devour.* The Message Bible says the devil is poised to pounce and would like nothing better than to catch us napping! We need to stay *on* guard so we don't get caught *off* guard.

It is interesting that Peter uses the analogy of a lion. You see, when a lion hunts prey in the jungle, he looks for a weak animal, one that has been separated from the herd, is injured, or very young. It's a quick and easy meal. God uses this imagery to show us how Satan stalks us. If we separate ourselves from people because of offense, injury, or just plain laziness, we set ourselves up as easy prey for the devil. When this happens, many people think it is God getting even with them for their past failures and bad choices. The truth is we are the ones who throw ourselves under the bus (or into the lion's mouth) by our choice to walk out of God's protection.

There is a real enemy out there but God has equipped us to stand against him by giving us the weapons we need for battle. To use them victoriously however, we must be able to recognize the sound of the enemy's voice, know what he looks like, and what his tactics are. If we do not realize that we have been equipped to stand and fight, we are like sitting ducks waiting to be his next meal.

God wants us to know we can unmask the enemy with the truth, calling his bluff and saying, "You can't do these things to me! I know who you are and I know who I am in Christ!" We certainly don't have this authority in our own strength. It is God who empowers us. Understanding this will help us see as God sees because we are wearing our God Glasses.

Ephesians 4:27-32 warns us not to give the enemy an opportunity in our lives, " ...*do not give the devil a foothold. He who has been stealing must steal no longer, but must work, doing something useful with his own hands, that he may have something to share with those in need. Do not let any unwholesome talk come out of your mouths, but only what is helpful for building others up according to their needs, that it may benefit those who listen. And do not grieve the Holy Spirit of God, with whom you were sealed for the day of redemption. Get rid of all bitterness, rage and anger, brawling and slander, along with every form of malice. Be kind and compassionate to one another, forgiving each other, just as in Christ God forgave you."*

Paul cautions us not to allow any unwholesome word to come out of our mouths but only what is kind, gentle and helpful for building up others. In other words, quit the put-downs, back-biting, and gossip. Those are hard ones, I know. I have gotten caught up in them in my own life. The devil tries to trip us up and sometimes we slip, but we certainly don't want to help him out when we know we can stop ourselves! Thankfully because I have the truth inside me, I'm quicker at catching myself today than I was yesterday, and I will be quicker still, tomorrow. When you stumble, get in the habit of immediately running to God for forgiveness and receiving His mercy. Don't give in to the devil's tactics. His plan is to use whatever he can against you so you will feel powerless all the time. Okay, so you blew it and you feel awful. Don't run away from God, He already knows what you did! Ask the Lord to help you not to do it again, say you are sorry and move on!

The Bible tells us a house divided cannot stand. Satan surely loves coming in, dividing our house and watching it fall. When we are living for God and doing what He has called us to do however, we are also opposing Satan—and *boy* does he hate it when that happens!

First John 3:8 (NLT) says, *"...the Son of God came to destroy the works of the devil."* What are the works of the devil? Anything that kills, steals, or destroys. Anything that gets you off course, keeps you from worshiping God, and prevents you from having a solid relationship with the Lord. The more you get to know God, the more you want to give Him every part of your life, the more you take God at His Word and trust Him, the more you act on Scripture and understand who you are in Christ—the greater the victory you will experience. While reading spiritual books is a good thing to do, you still need to spend time in the Bible, prayer, worship, and developing your personal friendship with God.

Satan works overtime to trap you in wrong thinking. If the devil had a mission statement it would read: "Deceive the followers of Jesus Christ. Dishonor God. Hate people. Steal, kill, and destroy everything and everybody I can get my hands on."

You have been given authority over the enemy. That is your position. Once you know this and are convinced of it, the devil won't be such a problem to you.

Those who bring conflict into our lives need to be seen through our God Glasses. Even though it looks as though they are the enemy, they are not. When we are angry or experiencing a fall out with someone, we need to see Satan behind the scenes tempting them and us to participate in his schemes, and enticing us to divide our houses.

Another strategy you can use to defeat the devil is found in Romans 12:21 (NKJ). *"Do not be overcome by evil, but overcome evil with good."* Let's see what that might look like. In Matthew 5:44 (NKJ), Jesus says, *"But I say to you, love your enemies, bless those who curse you, do good to those who hate you, and pray for those who spitefully use you and persecute you."* That's powerful! God has given you the Holy Spirit's power for facing the impossible. True, it can go against everything our flesh (and the enemy) wants us to do. Blessing someone who has just hurt us? Why that's ridiculous! Yes. Exactly. And that is exactly what God wants us to do because with God *all* things are possible.

When I was much younger, a lot less mature, and with little understanding of grace, I taught a Bible study and offended a woman in the class, who was an artist. I mean, I really goofed and seriously offended her. Now, rather than focusing on my mistake this time, I want you to pay attention to what she did in response to my insensitivity. The next time I saw her, she gave me a picture she had painted. I instantly saw that she was living the gospel, putting the Word into action, and blessing me—even though I had offended her. Her obedience to God in handling offense made an instant impression on my heart that I will never forget.

Years later, another opportunity for offense arose again, only this time I was on the receiving end. I immediately recalled that artist's godly response to me and put what I had learned from her into practice. I enjoy decorating candles, so I quickly bought a candle and decorated it with a ribbon and a cross as a gift to give the person. I'm not sure she ever realized she had offended me but that's not really the point. We don't always need to tell someone when they offend us. The point is to settle our feelings as the Lord leads. She may not have understood why I was giving a gift to her but I knew I was being obedient to God by blessing her.

You may have some unfinished business with God. Is there someone in your life you need to forgive, or say you are sorry to and ask forgiveness? Obey God. It's the most important thing you can do. You will not only be blessed by your obedience but the other person will also be blessed—and you will be shutting the door to the enemy in the situation.

Paul prayed in Ephesians that we would understand who God is and recognize His power inside of us. Our God Glasses help us see and understand that power, the same power that raised Christ from the dead. Wow! If we can truly grasp that, it will not only transform *our* lives but everyone else's, too!

Christ is seated above all principalities and powers. Jesus has taken His seat with the Father far above—not just above—but *far* above all principality, power, might and dominion, and every name that is named, not only in this age but also in that which is to come. Jesus is above it all. (See Ephesians 1:21)

Ephesians 1:22 (NKJ) goes on to tell us, *"And He put all things under His feet, and gave Him to be head over all things to the church..."* Get a picture of this: the same power that raised Christ from the dead, seated Him in heavenly places, and put everything under His feet is available to us as believers. We are not powerless against our enemy. We are strong in Him who strengthens us. Jesus has been made to be the head over all things. Everything is under His feet. There is nothing He can't handle.

Ephesians 2:6 (NKJ) says God *"...raised us up together, and has made us sit together in the heavenly places in Christ Jesus."* You may not be able to see that in your life right now but if you're a follower of Jesus Christ and you want Him to lead your life, His power lives inside of you. Choose to believe it. Exercise your faith and grow in the knowledge of what belongs to you in Him.

Our lives do not become a sweet-smelling bed of roses when we come to Christ. We still live in a corrupt world. However, anyone who puts their faith in Him will not be disappointed. When we come to Him, we find a peace that we have not experienced before.

You can find help through the power of Christ in you but first you have to choose. Put on your God Glasses and the choice will be easy! There is persecution all around us but Jesus has told us to be of good cheer because He has already overcome the world. What more do we need?

THE BIBLE
TELLS US TO
LOVE OUR
NEIGHBORS,
AND ALSO
OUR ENEMIES,
PROBABLY
BECAUSE
GENERALLY
THEY ARE THE
SAME PEOPLE.

–G. K. CHESTERTON

nine

seeing your health as
GOD SEES IT

I was raised in a denomination that taught me religion and religious traditions to follow but I was unaware that there could be much, much more. As an adult when I entered into a sincere relationship with Jesus, I discovered the joy of truly following Him. I became a borderline fanatic! Oh, how my family and friends could tell you stories! I have been a born-again Christian for more than thirty years now.

I admire gardeners. They have an eye for the beauty of creation, patience and tenacity, and they like to dig in their gardens for hours on end. While I don't personally relate to digging in dirt, I do love digging into God's Word! I am an avid student of the Bible. I can have more fun going through commentaries, dictionaries, and concordances than you could probably imagine. When I start digging, I feel like I'm on a great adventure with God discovering hidden treasure and all its wonders for hours at a time. As followers of Jesus, each of us represents a unique part of the Body of Christ. I believe my part is to share what I learn from studying the Bible with people who are hungry for more of God. It is a tremendous privilege that I have been passionate about since I first began my relationship with Him.

As we have discussed in previous chapters, there are two ways we can see: through our natural eyes or through our spiritual eyes. The first way provides limited perspective which can be skewed and may not line up with the truth in God's Word. The second way reveals the truth as it lines up with the infallible Word of God. In this chapter, I would like to share with you the truth about health and wholeness that I've learned from studying God's Word. Put on your God Glasses and I will show you in Scripture that it is God's will for you to experience health and healing in your spirit, soul, and body.

When we are born again we receive God's gift of salvation and begin a fresh new journey with Him. When we submit ourselves to His Lordship, He gives us eternal life—effective immediately! Some people think salvation means they are going to heaven, but that is not the actual definition of the word. It means more than that. Translated from the Greek word "sozo," salvation means "to save, deliver or protect (literally or figuratively)." (See Strong's Exhaustive Concordance.)

Sozo also means complete wholeness in the spirit. That wholeness is not limited to eternal life. Salvation in Jesus Christ offers deliverance from sin so we can experience God completely. It's as though He presents us with a great big beautiful gift package wrapped in a glorious ribbon with everything we need for healthy freedom in Christ neatly tucked inside.

As we discuss sozo, let's also look at the context of the word "saved" found in John 3:16-17 (NKJ). *"For God so loved the world that He gave His only begotten Son, that whoever believes in Him should not perish but have everlasting life. For God did not send His Son into the world to condemn the world, but that the world through Him might be saved* [sozo]."

Now let's look at the context of the word "healed" in Mark 5:23 (NKJ): *"...My little daughter lies at the point of death. Come and lay Your hands on her, so that she may be healed* [sozo], *and she will live."* The word healed is also translated from the Greek word sozo. Same word, different translations, but they essentially mean the same thing. Therefore to be "saved" is to be "healed," and vice versa.

Now let's look at another verse to further confirm this. Luke 8:35-36 (NKJ) says, *"Then they went out to see what had happened, and came to Jesus, and found the man from whom the demons had departed, sitting at the feet of Jesus, clothed and in his right mind. And they were afraid. They also who had seen it told them by what means he who had been demon-possessed was healed."* The word "healed" is once again translated from the word sozo. Another meaning of this word is "deliverance." In this verse, the word "healed" is synonymous with being delivered from demonic spirits.

So we see proof in three separate word translations with one inclusive meaning: God brings salvation, healing and deliverance through Jesus Christ. Jesus came to restore the world back to wholeness in spirit, soul *and* body.

In 3 John 2 (NKJ) Paul prays, *"Beloved, I pray that you may prosper in all things and be in health, just as your soul prospers."* The word "all" in this verse indicates God wants us to prosper and be healthy in *every* area of our lives.

Understanding that it is God's will for you to be healthy in spirit, soul and body is important for developing the faith to receive it. Faith says we can agree with God's Word for wholeness and healing whether we can see our healing right away or not! (See Hebrews 11:1.)

There are many people who believe they are going to heaven because they think being good will get them there. Tragically they leave Jesus out of the equation. In Mark 7, Jesus talks to a group of Pharisees, religious men who were so consumed with laws and rituals they didn't recognize Jesus as the Messiah. Those men were waiting to see if He would break any of their religious laws. In verse 13, Jesus tells them they are overtaken by their traditions to such a degree that they nullify the Word of God.

When I read this, I can understand how I had believed the religious traditions, rules, and laws in the church I grew up in that were not actually biblically based. As a young person, I was taught that I would go to heaven by being good. You can go to heaven by being good? How good do you have to be? How often? How long? Trying to earn your eternal reward based on performance carries a lot of pressure!

Then I discovered Ephesians 2:8-9 (NKJ). *"For by grace you have been saved through faith, and that not of yourselves; it is the gift of God, not of works, lest anyone should boast."* I'm not suggesting you throw out all traditions. Some traditions, like eating turkey and dressing on Thanksgiving or hanging stockings on the mantle at Christmas are fun and don't contradict God's Word.

A tradition can be a long-established custom or belief handed down from generation to generation. Sometimes an off-hand remark can become a tradition because it is spoken with authority and never checked against the Word of God.

God's Word is simple, but we humans make it complicated. People who don't wear their God Glasses may believe: a.) God has a plan and purpose for inflicting them with sickness; or b.) He's allowing them to endure sickness as His way of perfecting them.

When I hear people say their sickness is a good thing because they are growing closer to God, I just cringe. I don't know where that false belief came from but it is *not* in the Bible! John 10:10 says Jesus came so we could have life and have it more abundantly. It doesn't say we have to get sick first!

Have you ever had someone tell you that their chronic illness is a gift from the Lord and that it allows them to suffer with the sufferings of Christ? That's a twisting of Scripture. First of all, chronic illness is not a gift from the Lord, second Jesus was never chronically ill, and third, God does not make us sick! Sickness and disease came with the fall.

Have you heard this one? "I'm sick because God wants to teach me something." Oh my. Such human thinking—and completely off. Romans 8:28 promises us that God will use all things for good for those who love Him and are called to His purposes. What better way to use your time while you are flat on your back than to learn something about God and His Word. Good happens! But just because you gain insight and grow in love toward God while you're sick, doesn't mean He *caused* you to be sick just so He could teach you something.

The purpose of Scripture is identified for us in 2 Timothy 3:16 (NKJ). *"All Scripture is given by inspiration of God, and is profitable for doctrine, for reproof, for correction, for instruction in righteousness."* His Word can teach us without making us sick. Does that mean we can't learn while we're sick? No. God can teach us in every experience, if we will pay attention.

Throughout the gospels, Jesus taught people who He was and why He came. *"…God anointed Jesus of Nazareth with the Holy Spirit and power, and how He went around doing good and healing all who were under the power of the devil, because God was with Him.* (Acts 10:38)

If you believe something that does not line up with the truth of the Bible, you believe a lie that can cause God's Word not to work effectively in your life. You must question anything that tries to tell you that God has caused harm to one of His children, including you. If His Word tells us He is good (and it does tell us that) then He is good *all* the time. Everything He does for us is done in love and for our good because that is who God is. Put on your God Glasses so you can see beyond tradition and customary beliefs to discover the truth.

When God's Word is planted in your heart and watered with faith, it will produce a harvest in your life. The promises of God work when you practice them. If you follow traditions that contradict His Word, that's a very real problem that will hinder you from receiving all God has for you. Faith and doubt cannot coexist any more than light can coexist with darkness.

We're all familiar with the passage in the gospels where Jesus teaches His disciples how to pray. Some call it the Lord's Prayer and others call it the Our Father. In it, Jesus instructs us to pray that God's will to be done on earth just as it is in heaven. Is there sickness in heaven? Of course not! If there is no sickness in heaven, why would we ever think He would cause us to be sick here on earth? Nowhere in the New Testament does Jesus cause sickness in anyone, neither does he refuse to heal anyone who comes to Him for healing.

It is my prayer for you that as you study God's Word and keep your God Glasses on that you will be fully persuaded that healing is God's will. It's a good idea to be convinced *before* you get sick. When you know this truth and your body is attacked, you can apply your faith and rest assured that it is His will to heal you.

In the fourth chapter of Romans, the Apostle Paul tells us the story of Abraham's faith. God told Abraham he would become a father to many nations. That may not seem like a big deal to some people, but Abe was 100 years old. If that didn't make it unlikely enough, his wife Sarah was ninety! Abraham was wearing his God Glasses and didn't even blink when God gave him this promise. He believed what God told him. When we truly believe what God says is true, we will receive all of His promises.

You may remember God called Abraham friend. When you have a good friend, you hang out together and share intimately with each other. This is the kind of relationship Abraham had with God. God wants to have the same kind of relationship with you. Like Abraham, in order to believe God's promises, you need to become His friend, hang out with Him, and develop intimacy with Him. You do that by praying, reading His Word, and keeping your God Glasses on.

Are there ever exceptions to God's promises? No. There are no exceptions. Second Corinthians 1:20 (NKJ) tells us, *"For all the promises of God in Him are Yes, and in Him Amen, to the glory of God through us."* Can there be an exception to healing? Is there somebody *somewhere* that it really isn't God's will to heal? Is that possible? No! Why? Because God is not schizophrenic, that's why. He is neither double-minded nor does He change the one mind He has! Let's look at a few Scriptures to back this up. Malachi 3:6 (NKJ), *"...I am the Lord, I do not change..."* Numbers 23:19 (NKJ), *"God is not a man, that He should lie...";* and Romans 3:4 (NKJ), *"Certainly not! Indeed, let God be true but every man a liar. As it is written: 'That You may be justified in Your words, and may overcome when You are judged.'"*

God's Word is a sure foundation built on truth. Be assured you are not the one-in-a-million or even the one-in-a-*billion* person for whom it is not God's will to heal. God's will is to heal every person. In Exodus 15:26, God reveals who He is through His name. He says He is Jehovah Rapha, the God who heals.

In the New Testament, we know Jesus paid the price of our sin and sickness so we could experience total redemption. We don't have to try to talk God into healing us. He's already accomplished it on the cross and He's made it available to anyone who believes. Put on our God Glasses and see for yourself!

You may be asking yourself why healing doesn't always happen. There's another traditional way of thinking that can steal healing from us. It appears to be the right way to believe because there's *some* truth in it but it's not the whole truth. Referring to God's sovereignty, some of us have been told, "You never know what

God is going to do, or not do. He can do whatever He wants." While it is true God can do anything He wants, He will never go against His nature, character, or Word. His will to heal is not going to change. He never said healing is His will *sometimes*. It is His will *all* the time. He's either Jehovah Rapha or He is not. If you decide He is not Jehovah Rapha, it doesn't change the truth that He is! Psalm 138:2 says God will magnify His Word above His name. His Word is who He is. He is God Almighty—and God Almighty keeps His Word!

You may be wondering about Old Testament Scriptures that tell of God's wrath being poured out on disobedient people. How can that be if God is the same yesterday, today, and forever? Keep in mind the Israelites didn't have the perfect High Priest yet, so the earthly high priest would only be a temporary fix for the sinfulness of men and women. When they sinned and acted in total defiance to God, they had to pay for their sins by going to the temple and making animal sacrifices for their rebellion. There was never an end to the rebellion of His people. They sinned; they made a payment for their sin. Since the payments were not permanent, they needed to be repeated over and over. From the time of man's first sin with Adam and Eve in the Garden, God had been preparing a way to restore a friendship with His beloved creation. Jesus would be that answer once and for all.

In Hebrews 10:4 (NKJ) it says, *"For it is not possible that the blood of bulls and goats could take away sins."* It goes on to say in verses 8 through 10, *"Previously saying, 'Sacrifice and offering, burnt offerings, and offerings for sin You did not desire, nor had pleasure in them' (which are offered according to the law), then He said, 'Behold,*

I have come to do Your will, O God.' He takes away the first that He may establish the second. By that will we have been sanctified through the offering of the body of Jesus Christ once for all."

God is a just God. Where there is sin there has to be payment. He is the same God! He doesn't change. The almost-too-good-to-be-true news is what God did for the people He dearly loved; He sent Jesus to pay for sin once and for all. *"He Himself is the sacrifice that atones for our sins—not only our sins but the sins of all the world."* (1 John 2:2 NLT)

"For God so loved the world that He gave His one and only Son, that whoever believes in Him shall not perish but have eternal life." (John 3:16) We are reminded in John 17:3, *"Now this is eternal life: that they may know You, the only true God, and Jesus Christ, whom You have sent."* I believe healing is God's will for all of us today. I believe we can apply our faith to His Word and be healed. I believe in praying for the sick and expecting to see them healed.

I had a good friend who died too young. I don't know why she died but I do know she put her faith in God's Word up to her last breath. Does that mean God's will to heal is meaningless? No. It just means we don't know all the answers and we probably won't until we get to heaven. The important thing to remember is that God and His promises never change, regardless of our natural circumstances.

You may know someone who died even though you prayed for them to be healed. That may have caused a stumbling block in your faith in God's goodness. We can't base our faith on our circumstances; we base it on the unchangeable solid rock of God's Word. We may never know this side of heaven why someone doesn't get healed. Even when we don't have all the answers, we still know the Truth. There are things we do know even when we don't know everything. We do know God doesn't make anyone sick. It is not His character. Jesus showed us the Father's heart while here on earth, healing all who were oppressed of the devil.

Why is it whenever we can't explain tragedy, we blame it on God? "Oh, it must have been God's will." Surely we've lost our God Glasses somewhere because our picture of God is totally distorted! Let's look at John 10:10 (NKJ) again. *"The thief does not come except to steal, and to kill, and to destroy. I have come that they may have life, and that they may have it more abundantly."*

There is a traditional falsehood that seems to be spoken particularly after a young person dies. "God must have needed him in heaven." But God doesn't need anyone in heaven. It is His will for us to have long life on earth and then to spend eternity with Him in heaven. Look what it says in Proverbs 3:1-2 (AMP): *"My son, forget not my law or teaching, but let your heart keep my commandments; For length of days and years of life [worth living] and tranquility [inward and outward and continuing through old age till death], these shall they add to you."* In addition, Ephesians 6:2 promises God will bless you with long life for honoring your parents.

In Matthew 8:17 (NKJ) Jesus went about healing *"that it might be fulfilled which was spoken by Isaiah the prophet, saying, 'He Himself took our infirmities and bore our sicknesses.'"* Jesus fulfilled the prophesy Isaiah had spoken in the Old Testament. In 1 Peter 2:24 (NKJ) we read, *"...by whose stripes you are healed."* The word "stripes" refers to the stripes on Jesus' back where He had been whipped. He bore your sins, your pain, and your diseases.

You may not need physical healing in your body but your heart can be broken and you need emotional healing. God's will is for you to experience health and healing for your whole person. Sozo means wholeness! Jesus wants to heal your wounded heart.

In Luke 17:19 (NKJ), Jesus healed people and told them to *"...Arise and go your way. Your faith has made you well."* Several times in the New Testament Jesus says, *"It shall be done to you according to your faith."* Do you see the "according to your faith" part? That means we have a part to play in the manifestation of our healing. We take hold of the promise for healing by faith, by believing God and by keeping our God Glasses on.

Just as weightlifters know that repetitious exercise builds muscles, you can strengthen your faith to reach out and receive God's healing power by thinking continually about the healing promises found in God's Word—and by keeping those God Glasses on!

The bottom line is God wants us well and can heal us many different ways. Miracles happen. Many times in the gospels after Jesus healed blind eyes and deaf ears, He would say, "Go in peace. Your faith has made you whole."

Prayers for the sick often bring relief from pain, sickness and chronic illness. God uses doctors to heal us, too. Amazing medical discoveries and brilliant doctors reinforce this daily. He has provided them with wisdom and creativity so they can invent medicines and medical procedures to heal the human body. We are not to put our faith in doctors, however. Our faith is in our healer, The Great Physician. We put our faith and trust in Jehovah Rapha to guide the doctor through the healing direction He gives them. God is good and *He* will meet your need for healing, no matter which avenue it comes through.

There is only one instance recorded in Matthew 13:58 (NKJ) that said Jesus did not perform miracles. *"Now He did not do many mighty works there because of their unbelief."* He was in His hometown and the people did not have faith to believe "little Jesus, the carpenter's son" could be a miracle worker. Look at the significance of faith for healing.

You may feel weak in your faith right now but God has placed people in your life whose faith you can "borrow" to receive your healing. Ask them to pray for you. In the Book of James it says to call for the elders of the church and let them lay hands on the sick and they will recover.

Healing can also come through revelation from the Holy Spirit. I knew a farmer who was experiencing excruciating back pain and had been working out in the fields all day in the hot sun. He had prayed for God to heal his back but the pain continued. Finally, he received a revelation from the Holy Spirit who said, "You need to drink water." He started drinking water right away and almost immediately felt the pain go away! His back pain was from dehydration but he had been working so hard he hadn't realized he hadn't been drinking enough water. He followed the Holy Spirit's instructions and received his healing.

In a similar situation, I once had extreme shoulder pain while working at my computer. Like the farmer, I was praying for God to remove the pain but it wasn't leaving. Finally, I heard the Lord reveal the source of my problem—poor posture. I immediately changed the way I had been sitting and felt much better.

People have asked me to pray for their general health. They've also asked me to pray for specific needs and scheduled surgeries. Often I'll ask the Lord to fill the doctor or surgeon with wisdom and discernment so they can immediately diagnose the problem. I pray nothing goes undiscovered and that recovery will be supernaturally quickened. More often than not people can easily connect their faith to that type of prayer. You can pray this way too.

There will be times when the Lord gives you a special gift of faith for someone's healing that looks all but impossible in the natural. God may even ask you to pray to raise the dead. When that happens, trust Him to put His life-giving healing words in your mouth. After you've done your part, stand back and watch what the Lord does. Don't ever limit God!

Faith comes by hearing the Word of God. Strengthen and build up your faith by learning what God has to say about healing. Read it. Listen to it. Speak aloud His promises. Put on your God Glasses and call on Jehovah Rapha, your healer.

FAITH IS NOT BELIEF WITHOUT PROOF BUT TRUST WITHOUT RESERVATION.

—ELTON TRUEBLOOD

ten

how God
SEES PRAYER

10

Hanging up the phone, I wondered why I felt like I was missing something. Having just shared all the exciting things happening in my life with my two sisters, Chris and Colleen, I realized I hadn't stopped to ask them how they were doing, how their children were, or what was new in their lives. Instead, I had shared what was at the forefront of my mind: my excitement about my son, Andy's new home and my daughter, Amy's engagement. It had been a one-way conversation all about my family and me. It occurred to me at that point that my talks with God had been going the same way. I was doing all the talking and asking all the questions, but I was not giving Him a chance to answer. Apparently I just like to hear myself talk!

A monologue doesn't really build relationship. It delivers information but there is no allotted time for response from the listener. Prayer is our direct communication with God and is meant to be a two-way conversation, Spirit to spirit, heart to heart. One talks the other listens and each responds, gives, and receives.

Spending time with God is essential to building a strong, personal relationship with Him. It's an important part of our daily lives, or at least it should be. While there is no precise time of day or specific amount of time we are to pray, we *are* to pray. The Apostle Paul tells us in 1 Thessalonians 5:17 to pray without ceasing. Praying non-stop is keeping God on your mind, thinking about Him, and talking with Him throughout the day. Even as you drive, you can talk to Him as if He is in the seat next to you. The more intimate your relationship with Him, the more you will want to grab hold of this sublime privilege.

Have you ever bought a computer that had software you had never used before? If you are like me, I expect software to think like me so I try what I think should work. Usually I don't get the results I want until I click on the "Help" menu. The same is true in prayer. If you are not getting results, consider how you are praying. Maybe there's a better way. Keep your God Glasses on while you pray and watch what happens. Your ideas on prayer will turn into God's plan for prayer as He guides you.

Spending time in prayer gives you the opportunity to tell God how much you love Him and how great He is. It also gives you the opportunity to thank Him for what He has done for you and for others. You can say, "Thank you Lord, for loving the people in my life more than I love them. Your love is beyond measure and my limited human love is small in comparison. Thank you, Jesus, for dying for each one of them and for providing eternal life for every single person in the world." Even if you are going through a difficult trial, when you put your God Glasses on you will see the situation as God sees it. Problems are no big deal to God.

Prayer includes being sorry for your mistakes and looking to God to help you overcome weak areas. Know that He will forgive you immediately and won't need time to think about the situation. He wants you to walk in the freedom of His forgiveness.

As you talk to Him, you can also release the hurts you've received and the offenses you've taken, placing all of it in His loving hands. *"And when you stand praying, if you have anything against anyone, forgive him, so that your Father in heaven may also forgive you your sins."* (Mark 11:25 NKJ)

Sometimes it isn't easy to forgive someone without still secretly hoping they get what you think they deserve. The wonder of it all is you can also tell *that* to God and by an act of your will you can choose to forgive them anyway. God already knows what's in your heart. That's what true relationship is.

During your conversations with God, forgive those who have spitefully used you and then ask God to bless them. Yes, that's right, bless them. Thank Jesus, literally, that you don't have to be perfect to approach God—or none of us ever could. He wants you to share your heart with Him so He can teach you more about His ways. Nothing will block our spiritual growth more profoundly than an unforgiving spirit. It takes God Glasses to sincerely pray for others.

When wounds and offenses happen, our forgiveness shuts the door so the enemy can't use the opportunity for his demonic purposes. Sometimes it's easy to forgive, and once done, it is finished. Other times it's like peeling the proverbial onion—we forgive with each layer until the fumes are gone and the foothold is fully removed from our hearts.

When you have a healthy relationship with someone, you approach him or her confidently knowing you can talk freely, sharing your heart openly with the each other. God wants you to approach Him the same way. First John 5:14 says, *"This is the confidence we have in approaching God: that if we ask anything according to His will, He hears us."*

Reading the Word and thinking about it builds the foundation of prayer life. It is God's desire that you and I pray according to His Word. Knowing what is written in the Bible is essential for understanding His nature and character. Effective prayer comes when His words become our words. His will is revealed in His Word. In prayer, we need to agree with what God has already said. Keeping your God Glasses on helps you focus on God and pray His will.

Sometimes we don't get the desired outcome in prayer that we were expecting and it seems like God isn't listening, but He is! He watches over His Word to perform it but He doesn't perform every word that you utter. God wants you to pray boldly according to His will which is found in His Word. When His will becomes your prayer, you can confidently look forward to the results He has planned. Your God Glasses will help you determine what God's Word has for you when you look to the Holy Spirit for understanding.

You may think there's no such thing as praying wrongly, but there is. God knows the problems in our lives. Sometimes we can become so overwhelmed with a problem that our "prayer" is just a rehash of every ugly detail, magnifying the problem, and agreeing with the enemy—never waiting for God's wisdom or answer. We vent, and then say "Amen!" That is not prayer. That's whining. So, then as an afterthought we add, "Lord, I am happy to go through this, if it is Your will." These are not effective prayers. Nothing has been accomplished except that we probably made the devil smile. What's the point? In effect, we are telling God that the problem is bigger than Him. We add in a loophole in case the prayer goes unanswered, so then we can accept our problems as if they were God's intention from the beginning.

The Bible says God will give you the desires of your heart. In other words, when you are following the Lord, He will answer your requests. As your heart moves more toward Him, He will direct your desires. As long as the desires of your heart are not contrary to His Word, you can bet they are from Him.

People believe that everything that happens is God's will and everything that occurs is for a reason—another traditional belief that is not found in Scripture but is very popular among religious people. Second Peter 3:9 (NCV) tells us, *"The Lord is not slow in doing what He promised—the way some people understand slowness. But God is being patient with you. He does not want anyone to be lost, but He wants all people to change their hearts and lives."* This verse shows us God's will for people is that no one is lost. We know that is not always the case, so His desires do not always come to pass. This free will thing trips up our religious thinking. It's so important to keep our God Glasses on when we pray and read God's Word. Our prayers need to be in agreement with what God has already revealed through His Word. We can't assume religious sounding prayers are God's will. Knowing what God said and understanding our authority will strengthen our confidence to boldly approach God in prayer.

God wants you to come to Him in prayer with your desires. You are to make your requests known to God. He is a Father who enjoys providing for His children. Your God Glasses will help you sift through traditional beliefs and zero in on God's will for your life. Praying according to His Word keeps you from praying wrongly. Understanding God's will allows you to pray confidently.

In 1 John 5:14-15 (NKJ) we read: *"Now this is the confidence that we have in Him, that if we ask anything according to His will, He hears us. And if we know that He hears us, whatever we ask, we know that we have the petitions that we have asked of Him."* God says if we pray according to His will, He hears us. I think that's awesome! I like praying God's will and knowing He hears me. It means I agree with Him—not that He needs my opinion—but He likes my agreement. We honor Him when we pray according to His will.

Finally, as you commune with God in prayer, be sure to give Him a chance to speak to your heart in everything you pray. Allow a free-flowing conversation from your heart to His and back again. Bask in His presence and let your heart worship Him throughout your time with Him. The more you do, the closer your relationship will be with the One who loves you with remarkable, unconditional love.

I love the names of God. He reveals Himself in His names. In Exodus 15:26, God refers to Himself as Jehovah Rapha which means "The God who Heals." So when I pray for someone who needs healing, I can boldly ask God for it because I know it is His will. He's made it clear in the Old and New Testaments, therefore I'm convinced!

When you pray, if you think God is a distant God who may or may not be within earshot of your voice, put on your God Glasses. He is right there with you and absolutely loves spending time with you in One-on-one conversation. If you have asked Him to be your best friend, He lives inside of you and He has promised not to ever leave you or forget you. In the gospel of John, Jesus says His sheep (that's you and me!) know His voice and the voice of a stranger they do not follow. When you wear your God Glasses, you can recognize the laws and traditions imposed on you that aren't true to God's Word. Seeing with God's perspective is seeing it God's way and not man's way.

I'm on the prayer team at my church where I have the privilege of joining my faith with others to pray. One of the first things I ask is, "What would you like me to pray?" Doesn't that make sense? We need to know specifically what the need is before we can pray and agree in prayer. We all want good results. Some people come needing healing and when they do I try to locate where they are in their faith so I can agree with them. Jesus said, *"It shall be done to you according to your faith."* Someone may want prayer for a surgery they're about to have. So I pray the doctors will have wisdom and the surgery goes well. My job isn't to judge the level of their faith; it's to agree with what God's Word says about their situation. God wants to bring answers to their prayers and His answers will always agree with His word.

Once I prayed with a woman who wanted me to agree in prayer that the offer she made on a house she wanted would be accepted. There was a time in my life when I would agree with people on just about anything, which was totally ridiculous!

Instead, I asked her if she thought her offer was fair. She hesitated and then told me the price she was actually willing to pay. I told her I couldn't agree that her offer would be accepted if she wasn't sure it was a fair one, but I could pray she would find the right house for the right price. She agreed and then we prayed.

Paul gives an excellent model of prayer in the first chapter of Ephesians. *"For this reason, ever since I heard about your faith in the Lord Jesus and your love for all the saints, I have not stopped giving thanks for you, remembering you in my prayers. I keep asking that the God of our Lord Jesus Christ, the glorious Father, may give you the Spirit of wisdom and revelation, so that you may know Him better. I pray also that the eyes of your heart may be enlightened in order that you may know the hope to which He has called you, the riches of His glorious inheritance in the saints, and His incomparably great power for us who believe. That power is like the working of His mighty strength."* (Ephesians 1:15-19) That's why we pray for people, especially believers. They may not be living as they should be, but when we pray God's Word over them, it's like shooting God's arrow at a bull's-eye in the spirit. God's Word is effective, gets right to the point and accomplishes what He intends.

Another place Paul prays is found in Ephesians 3:14-19. *"For this reason I kneel before the Father, from whom His whole family in heaven and on earth derives its name. I pray that out of His glorious riches He may strengthen you with power through His Spirit in your inner being, so that Christ may dwell in your hearts through faith. And I pray that you, being rooted and established in love, may have power, together with all the saints, to grasp how wide and long and high and deep is the love of Christ, and to know this love that surpasses knowledge—that you may be filled to the measure of all the fullness of God.*" I love this prayer! I pray it over people all the time because it addresses their inner man. When you know who you are in Christ, you receive strength and confidence to pray as He wants you to pray for people.

Early in my life I was taught to storm the gates of heaven and ask God to send revival. Then I straightened my God Glasses and realized we didn't have to beg God to send revival. He wants revival more than we do! We can ask God to change us so we will be more like Him and then we will start seeing revival outbreaks all around us. When we begin to move like God, people will notice and want what we have. They'll want to follow His move.

We often pray and ask God to get the devil off our backs, but when we study the New Testament we see that Jesus already destroyed the works of the devil. So why does the devil seem to just run rampant everywhere? People are not taking their rightful, God-given positions. In Ephesians 1, we read about the power in us. It's the same power that was in Jesus when He was raised from the dead and seated at the right hand of His Father, placing everything under His feet. In Ephesians 2:6, Paul goes on to tell us that we also are seated with Jesus with everything under our feet! We have been given godly authority. We just need to keep our God Glasses on, believe it, and act on it.

The devil whispers lies in people's ears. They buy into those lies and submit their wills to Satan. We need to ask God to give people a spirit of wisdom and revelation into the knowledge of God, and then they will be able to use the authority they have in Him to render the devil powerless in their lives.

In 2 Corinthians 4:3-4 (NKJ), Paul gives us a glimpse into the hearts of those who have not committed their lives to God. *"But even if our gospel is veiled, it is veiled to those who are perishing, whose minds the god of this age has blinded, who do not believe, lest the light of the gospel of the glory of Christ, who is the image of God, should shine on them."* This Scripture provides insight into how the enemy covers people's faces with a veil so they are blinded to the truth, causing them to be lost. Take the initiative to pray for the removal of this veil so they will see the truth. God has given you power over the enemy through Jesus Christ to command it. What happens when the veil is removed from their eyes? They are able to make decisions for themselves which will bring them eternal life by choosing Jesus. It doesn't guarantee they will make all the right decisions but they won't be blind to the gospel of Jesus Christ anymore. You can't pray against someone's will because God gives each of us a free will to choose. They have a right to choose for themselves.

Another prayer you can pray for the lost is found in Luke 10:2 (NKJ). *"...The harvest truly is great, but the laborers are few; therefore, pray the Lord of the Harvest to send out laborers into His harvest."* I often pray according to this Scripture for people who have either wandered away from God or who have never had a relationship with Him. I pray for God, the Lord of the Harvest, to send believers to share the Good News in a way they will understand. I believe the hearts of those who hear the message will be ready to receive, in Jesus' Name.

Don't be surprised or offended if those you love are reluctant to receive the gospel from you. Sometimes you can be too close for them to hear what you have to say. In other words, it may not be the message, but the messenger. Don't worry! God has other people in mind who can reach your loved ones. You are not the only tool in His toolbox.

When I give my time and resources to others, I believe God is using me to answer someone's prayer. In the same way, you can be someone's answer to prayer. As I sow into someone's life, I become a laborer in their harvest. I also know that what I sow, I'm going to reap and I know God will bless me in my own life. I know He's sending people to those I care about so they can hear the voice of God, the veil will be removed from their eyes, they will know the truth and be able to make their own choice. I don't know when it will happen, but I also don't grow weary or lose heart because I know God is faithful to His Word.

Be confident in Jesus Christ as you put your trust in the One who is able to do everything He promises. And, keep your God Glasses on so you can watch Him answer your prayers.

IN PRAYER,
IT IS BETTER
TO HAVE
A HEART
WITHOUT
WORDS
THAN WORDS
WITHOUT
HEART.

–JOHN BUNYUN

eleven

doubt will smear
YOUR GLASSES

Have you been practicing wearing your God Glasses? Great! Uh, …wait a minute. What's that stuff all over your lenses? It looks …well, greasy. How did it get there? What is it?

Oh no. It's doubt. Doubt causes you to question whether or not God will keep His Word to you. Does He really have your back? Can you truly find rest in Him? Doubt blurs your vision or you wouldn't need to ask those questions. Why? It's like putting grease on your lenses. Doubt fogs your view. Unless you remove doubt completely, you won't be able to focus clearly.

Did you have a lousy day yesterday? Restless night tossing, turning …churning your problems? Are you fearful of what today has in store? Did you get up this morning thinking, "I don't want to have a day like yesterday ever again! I'll make sure I wear my God Glasses this time. Now, …where did I put them?"

If you've been in a state of unrest lately, feeling anxious, fearful, and doubting that God will do all He says He can, you may have laid your God Glasses down somewhere and now you can't remember where you put them. When was the last time you saw them? Without your Glasses, you are filtering life through the lenses of your five natural senses. Your perception is off.

Fear gives birth to doubt. We see this in Matthew 14. After a long day teaching the crowds, Jesus told His disciples to get into a boat and go across the sea to the other side. After several hours sailing, they found themselves being battered by high winds and waves in a life-threatening storm. They were scared out of their wits and weren't sure they were going to make it to the shore. *"Now in the fourth watch of the night Jesus went to them, walking on the sea. And when the disciples saw him walking on the sea, they were troubled, saying, 'It is a ghost!' And they cried out for fear. But immediately Jesus spoke to them, saying, 'Be of good cheer! It is I; do not be afraid."* (Matthew 14:25-27 NKJ) If the disciples had been wearing their God Glasses, they would have recognized Jesus when He came to rescue them. Instead, fear gripped their hearts and drained them of their faith.

Peter must have had his God Glasses on when he accepted Jesus' invitation to walk on the water but when he got distracted by the huge, churning waves all around him, he lost his nerve and started to sink. Perhaps his God Glasses were blown off by the high winds and when he looked at the situation with his natural eyes, he panicked. Jesus, his answer, was standing right in front of him, but fear had given birth to doubt, instantly clouding Peter's vision. As he began to sink, he cried out to the Savior for help. *"And immediately Jesus stretched out His hand and caught him, and said to him, 'O you of little faith, why did you doubt?'"* (Matthew 14:31 NKJ)

God says, "I will never leave you or forget about you." We need to cooperate with Him by reaching out to grasp what His extended hand is offering. That's how we engage our faith and activate the promises in His Word. Second Corinthians 1:20 (NKJ) tells us, *"For all the promises of God in Him are Yes, and in Him Amen, to the glory of God through us."* God answers "Yes" to the things He has promised in His Word but you have to believe He wants you to have them so you can receive them.

Mark 10:46-52 is a great "Yes" example. *"...a blind man, Bartimaeus (that is, the Son of Timaeus), was sitting by the roadside begging. When he heard that it was Jesus of Nazareth, he began to shout, 'Jesus, Son of David, have mercy on me!' Many rebuked him and told him to be quiet, but he shouted all the more, 'Son of David, have mercy on me!' Jesus stopped and said, 'Call him.' So they called to the blind man, 'Cheer up! On your feet! He's calling you.' Throwing his cloak aside, he jumped to his feet and came to Jesus. 'What do you want me to do for you?' Jesus asked him. The blind man said, 'Rabbi, I want to see.' 'Go,' said Jesus, 'your faith has healed you.' Immediately he received his sight and followed Jesus along the road."*

Everyone knew Bartimaeus was blind. Jesus knew. The disciples knew. The crowds of people who saw him day after day knew. So why did Jesus ask, "What can I do for you?" What was really going on here? Jesus was giving Bartimaeus the opportunity to reach out and receive his healing. He wanted him to use his faith. He was offering him the chance to participate in a miracle. Bartimaeus knew Jesus was his healer. It wasn't enough he was in the right place at the right time, Jesus wanted him to actively participate with his faith. He expects the same from you and me.

There is another Scripture that further illustrates God's "Yes." Mark tells us about the woman with the issue of blood in Mark 5:25-34 (NKJ). *"Now a certain woman had a flow of blood for twelve years, and had suffered many things from many physicians. She had spent all that she had and was no better, but rather grew worse. When she heard about Jesus, she came behind Him in the crowd and touched His garment. For she said, 'If only I may touch His clothes, I shall be made well.' Immediately the fountain of her blood was dried up, and she felt in her body that she was healed of the affliction. And Jesus, immediately knowing in Himself that power had gone out of Him, turned around in the crowd and said, 'Who touched My clothes?' But His disciples said to Him, 'You see the multitude thronging You, and You say, "Who touched Me?"' And He looked around to see her who had done this thing. But the woman, fearing and trembling, knowing what had happened to her, came and fell down before Him and told Him the whole truth. And He said to her, 'Daughter, your faith has made you well. Go in peace, and be healed of your affliction.'"* (Mark 5: 25-34 NKJ)

This woman had the faith to believe if she touched the hem of Jesus' garment, she would be healed. She had heard of Jesus and had so much faith in His power, she was determined to do whatever it took to reach Him. She didn't need one-on-one time with the Master. Just touching the hem of His garment would do.

You've got to picture the scene. There was a huge crowd around Jesus. They all wanted to be near Him to hear Him speak. They didn't yet know He was the Messiah but they had heard about the miracles He did. This woman was no different. She just had to get to Him! She knew where to get her healing.

According to Levitical law, this woman should not have been outside because she could have contaminated everyone. Nevertheless, she stepped out in faith, taking an enormous risk in a last-ditch effort and hope of being healed by Jesus. Can you see her moving desperately through the crowd, pushing past people until she finally reaches out and touches The Healer? Can you imagine the look on her face when she knew she had been healed? What caused the power to go out of Jesus and heal this woman? She certainly wasn't wearing smeared God Glasses. She saw her healing clearly. She believed and she received.

Fear is like a magnifying glass. It makes any difficult circumstance appear larger than God and diverts our attention away from God's answer to our problem. In Numbers 13, Moses sent twelve spies to check out the Promised Land to determine what they were up against. When they returned, all twelve reported the same thing: there were giants in the land. What their natural eyes had seen was true. There *were* giants in the land!

Fear gripped ten of the twelve spies and somewhere along that journey, they lost their God Glasses and predicted the worst possible scenarios for going into the land God had promised them. Never mind they had already walked the desert for forty years! Forget the fact that their shoes never wore out, they never went hungry, and they always arrived safely at each stopping place. Now suddenly they were afraid to enter the land flowing with milk and honey that God had promised. Go figure!

Two of the twelve spies, Joshua and Caleb, kept their God Glasses on and saw the land as God did. They didn't deny the facts.

They acknowledged there were giants in the land but they also believed they could overcome any adversity. They believed God's truth. They made God's promise the focus of their attention. The Lord delights in us when we have an attitude like this.

What needs do you have today? Tell Jesus. Ask Him, believing He will give you an answer. Tell Him you know He is willing and able to give you anything you need. Doubt is defeated as you act on what you have read in God's Word and as you talk about God's promises. Take hold of His promises by faith. Receive what you cannot see in the natural, until it comes to pass.

I remember driving through a snow storm in St. Louis, Missouri in near whiteout conditions. The snow was coming down so hard I could barely see the road in front of me. I had read driver safety tips for situations like this and remembered the warning not to pull over on the side of the road or you could end up as the first link in the chain of a multi-car accident. So I made sure my lights were on and pressed myself closer to the steering wheel, hoping to be able to see enough to stay in my own lane. The windshield wipers beat furiously against the oncoming snow, which was now coming down even harder than before. Suddenly, the sound of a horn screaming at me from a car headed straight for me caused me to swerve back into my own lane. Without warning, I had drifted into the opposite lane smack into oncoming traffic! Relying on my own eyesight had not been enough to protect me. My vision and my judgment had been dangerously off! Dirty God Glasses can have the same effect. We may think we are on the right track but we will never stay on God's path with faulty vision. Clean God Glasses allow us to rest in the Lord as we trust Him to keep us on His path.

Whether you are in crisis or not, because you believe in Christ, His gift to you is His rest. *"For we who have believed do enter that rest..."* (Hebrews 4:3 NKJ) Staying in bed all day with the covers over your head, refusing to deal with a challenging situation is not rest, it is depression. You receive God's rest by what you see in His Word through your God Glasses, not by what you see with your natural eyes. You choose to enter into His rest by believing in Him. It's achieved when you come to Him certain He is trustworthy and His Word is true. *"And the peace of God, which surpasses all understanding, will guard your hearts and minds through Christ Jesus."* (Philippians 4:7) His peace is beyond our understanding because we can't get there without Him. It's not based on feelings or emotions. When you are in His rest, you will have His supernatural peace in the midst of a storm, even when the winds of chaos and fear are whirling around you like a winter blizzard.

"...faith and patience inherit the promises." (Hebrews 6:12 NKJ) Have faith and be patient, just like the woman with the issue of blood. She waited twelve agonizing years for her healing. Rely on your God Glasses to help you see your answer in the spirit, even before you see it in the natural. Trust God to do what He says He will.

Doubt contradicts faith forcing you to see a situation based on uncertainty, disregarding God's Word. Faith, on the other hand, presses through to see in the spirit realm according to God's Word.

Doubt can hinder the future God has planned for you.

Decide today you are going to believe His Word no matter what your circumstances are. God said He will never leave you or forsake you. That's a promise! God loves you so much and wants the very best for you.

From now on, let God's Word be more real to you than anything you face. Add your faith to His Word and wipe doubt off your God Glasses so you can see clearly, starting right now.

There. That's better.

Wow. You're looking mighty fine in those God Glasses of yours! No more running into brick walls or falling off porches. Yep, you're looking good, looking smart. Everything about you says "class."

FAITH IS TO BELIEVE WHAT WE DO NOT SEE, AND THE REWARD OF THIS FAITH IS TO SEE WHAT WE BELIEVE.

–AUGUSTINE

twelve

broken
GLASSES

God Glasses can break, not because God didn't make them strong enough, but because we can weaken them by our actions or inactions, our beliefs and our unbeliefs. God Glasses can be broken by our wrong choices.

Have you ever noticed someone wearing broken glasses temporarily repaired with a safety pin or tape? Sad. Regular glasses can come loose at the hinge making it difficult to keep them on our nose, or we drop them and the lenses get cracked. Either way, broken glasses are difficult to use and give us a distorted view of things until they can be fully repaired.

The same is true for broken God Glasses. When the hinge is broken, they sit lopsided on our face, usually over just one eye. Wow. That's a weird perspective! Trying to see through cracked lenses is a bit like looking through a kaleidoscope and expecting to be able to read. Squinting doesn't help much. I can almost feel the headache coming on from the eye stress! Have you ever tried to look into a broken mirror? Like a Picasso painting, your eyes are not where they should be and your nose is in two different places. Nothing looks normal. That's what it's like trying to see with broken God Glasses.

We've seen what life can look like without our God Glasses. Now let's look at some choices and situations that end up breaking the God Glasses we have.

Without question, we live in a busy world full of distractions. Our calendars are full and our commitments are many. Attempting to make it through the day, we can take our eyes off Jesus and pay more attention to our circumstances. This does not mean we don't love God or won't spend eternity with Him, but it does mean we can foolishly take a break from God and push His Word aside, tossing our Glasses into the nearest drawer with a bunch of other stuff piled on top of them that ends up bending the frames.

Perhaps like the prodigal son, you've left home in rebellion to go off into the world and do your own thing. That's not a good place to be, but there is hope! If you have strayed from the truth of God's Word, you need to know that you have a loving Father who will welcome you back with outstretched arms. Nothing pleases the Father more than being reunited with His children and He will be delighted to hand you the God Glasses you left behind. He wants you to see clearly again!

Wounds, traumatic events, and tragedies can be devastating on your perspective. One moment you can be waltzing through life with everything going well, then suddenly, *wham!* The shock of unexpected tragedy or trauma tries to take you out and your Glasses fly off your face and break.

Has someone deeply wounded you through an unforgivable act perpetrated against you, viciously stepping on your God Glasses? Do you believe that holding on to unforgiveness will protect you from ever being hurt like that again? Do you pretend as though that person no longer exists and you have erased them from your life? Your God Glasses may have been stomped into the ground but they are not beyond repair. Take your wounds and your broken Glasses to God and forgive the person who has done the terrible damage. Jesus desperately wants to heal you, to restore your godly perspective, and yes, even that relationship. In the moment you release the offender with your forgiveness, your wounds will begin healing and your God Glasses will be restored, better than new.

Suffering great loss can result in broken Glasses. Have you lost a loved one? Your spouse or child? The sorrow of your heart can feel like a bottomless pit that can never be filled. No matter how hard you try to get through the day, you can't seem to see through the fog of grief. Your God Glasses have been shattered along with your heart. You may try to wear them hoping no one will notice they are broken, but the fog just won't go away. Pour out your broken heart to Jesus. He grieves with you at your loss. He will listen to everything you need to say. Tell Him all the things you feel. If you have anger, tell Him. If you have questions, ask Him. He will be there with you holding you in His arms and feeling your pain with you. He loves you with an everlasting love and tenderly wants to comfort you.

Matthew 15:7 reveals some ways our God Glasses can get broken. *"You hypocrites! Isaiah was right when he prophesied about* you: 'These people honor Me with their lips, but their hearts are far from Me. They worship Me in vain; their teachings are but rules taught by men.'"

Our God Glasses will not function properly if we are just going through the motions of Christianity. Going to church on Sunday for the social benefits alone is not a relationship builder with Jesus. Neither is secretly timing the sermon or counting the minutes until we can leave. Jesus wants us to enter into true worship with our eyes on Him and our hearts pouring out our love for Him. If we are more concerned with doing our best imitation of holiness, all the while peeking to see if everyone is admiring how holy we look during worship, our focus is going in the wrong direction. Presenting an 8 x 10 glossy of what we perceive is a good Christian face, smiling and saying nice things to people so they remember we showed up, then talking behind their backs all week does not honor Jesus. This is what Jesus called being a hypocrite. Jesus wants a real relationship with you and with me. Stop pretending. Pursue Him. Get to know Him. Learn from Him and you will be blessed.

Have you labeled Christians as hypocrites because something happened in your life that distorted the way you see people who profess to love God? Perhaps you really don't want anything to do with "Church" anymore because you believe Christians just talk the talk but don't walk the walk. So, let me get this straight, you've based your opinion of God on your imperfect view of those who claim to belong to Him? People are *not* perfect, but I'm sure you didn't need me to tell you that! You know it's true. People will make mistakes and disappoint you. As believers in

Jesus, we strive to represent Him in a manner that brings Him pleasure but we are human and we are still going to goof. The important thing is not to put people on a pedestal. They will just fall off. Jesus said, "Follow Me." He didn't say, "Follow them." He is our perfect role model. No one else comes close.

When a church leader falls in sin, the people of the congregation can be really hurt. Suffering from extreme disappointment, their world shaken, they may wonder aloud, "If he couldn't get it right, what makes me think that I ever will?" Some people end up blaming the Church as a whole, never to return, choosing instead to wander aimlessly as lone sheep rather than risk being disappointed by a fellow Christian again.

Mahatma Gandhi once said, "I would have become a Christian until I met one. If that's what Christianity looks like, I don't want any part of it. I like your Christ. I don't like your Christians. Your Christians are so unlike your Christ." Has someone from church offended you and now you don't want to go anymore? Has a church leader you respected fallen in sin and now you are a lone sheep walking in judgment of God's flock? Have you alienated yourself from the Church? Proverbs 18:1 (NAS) says, *"He who separates himself seeks his own desire, He quarrels against all sound wisdom."* If this is you, your emotions need healing. God made you to be in fellowship with Him and with other believers. He wants to mend relationships among His people so their vision can be restored. If your God Glasses have been cracked because of a church leader's behavior, seek to be restored with other Christians. Christians aren't perfect but Jesus still died for us anyway.

As I was talking with a friend one day, she shared with me a wrong belief she carried as a child that broke her God Glasses until she learned the truth and they could be repaired. As a young girl, she lived in fear that if she were to die before she told God she was sorry for each and every one of her sins, hell would be her destination. One day she came home to an empty house and thought Jesus had returned and taken everyone but her to heaven because she had sin in her life she had not confessed yet. That is so *sad*! Can you imagine that poor little girl's horror? A young child living in fear of going to hell? That is not an accurate representation of God. The Bible says we won't go to hell if we receive Jesus' free gift of salvation and choose to follow Him. Ephesians 2:9 tells us that no one can say they earned eternal life.

Living in a place of fear and condemnation won't bring you closer to God. It can weaken and eventually break your God Glasses. "Did I do something wrong today?" That constant, un-achievable demand for perfection will turn into anger, bitterness, or flat-out giving up. Living a perfect, sinless life is impossible this side of heaven. Only Jesus lived a sinless life and He knows we aren't perfect. He knows our mistakes mount up daily. When we are sold out for Jesus, however, sin just isn't fun anymore! Once we can correctly see all He has for us and receive it by faith we want to walk with Him and live out His Word in our lives.

Judgmental, self-deprecating thoughts lead to frustration and confusion and you will find that you are judging others as harshly as you judge yourself. Change how you think by transforming your mind. *"And do not be conformed to this world, but be transformed by the renewing of your mind, that you may prove what is that good and acceptable and perfect will of God."* (Romans 12:2 NKJ) As your mind gets a makeover from the Word of God, His Word will become more real to you, then you'll be able to give yourself and others a break.

God wants to set you free from fear and condemnation today. It is His will and His desire. He wants you to know His truth. You may not feel this freedom in your heart right away. You might be able to comprehend it with your mind but your heart just isn't grabbing hold of it yet. But I'm telling you, hang in there! Stick with it! Be persistent with God and His Word. He will bring you to a place where your heart and head are in agreement. He is the Good Shepherd and He leads His sheep—He is leading you right now. He loves you, you know. Learn to love yourself. It's hard to love others if you don't love yourself first. So go ahead, give yourself a great big hug!

Are you having difficulty relating to God the Father? Does He seem miles and miles away, too distant for you to reach? Unresolved, painful, home-life issues with your earthly father can cause you to believe that your heavenly Father will treat you the same way. Those issues can hold you in the past and keep you from enjoying the present.

Some people come into God's kingdom without ever having known their earthly fathers. They don't have an understanding of what a father-daughter or father-son relationship looks like or acts like. That lack of relationship understanding can also cause you to feel distant with God the Father. Be encouraged! You can tell your heavenly Father about your relationship concerns and ask Him to teach you how you can draw nearer to Him as His child.

You don't have to allow your past to control your present or your future. You can release it into God's hands. God looks into your heart and sees your pain. He knows what you have gone through. He gathered the tears you cried when you cried them. You may want to ask Him, "Why, God?" or "How could You have allowed that to happen to me?" You can even ask Him where He was when you went through what you did. The truth is God has been and always will be with you. He loves you very much and understands what you've been through. Trust Him. He is very good at what He does—He's a wonderful Father.

God gave you a creative imagination. If you allow it to run wild, slathered in negativity, imagining the worst possible scenarios, it can slowly destroy you. You can use your imagination for good as easily as you can for bad. Let's try it right now. Imagine what a perfect father would look like. Would he always be there for you and care about every detail of your life? Could you confide your innermost thoughts, fears, and desires to him? Would it delight him to give you gifts? Would you be the most precious child he could ever hope for? Are you the apple of his eye? You just painted a picture of Father God. He is exceedingly great and He is waiting for you to discover who He is and what He wants to do for you in your life.

· Paul talks about the freedom of letting go of the past in Philippians 3:7-14. *"But whatever was to my profit I now consider loss for the sake of Christ. What is more, I consider everything a loss compared to the surpassing greatness of knowing Christ Jesus my Lord, for whose sake I have lost all things. I consider them rubbish, that I may gain Christ and be found in Him, not having a righteousness of my own that comes from the law, but that which is through faith in Christ—the righteousness that comes from God and is by faith. I want to know Christ and the power of His resurrection and the fellowship of sharing in His sufferings, becoming like Him in His death, and so, somehow, to attain to the resurrection from the dead. Not that I have already obtained all this, or have already been made perfect, but I press on to take hold of that for which Christ Jesus took hold of me. Brothers, I do not consider myself yet to have taken hold of it. But one thing I do: Forgetting what is behind and straining toward what is ahead, I press on toward the goal to win the prize for which God has called me heavenward in Christ Jesus.*" Can you see what that looks like? Letting the past go and pushing forward with anticipation for what God has for you? There's a prize! Isn't that amazing?

Have you ever gone to a carnival and played one of the games there? Your goal is to win that great big prize on the back wall. Deep down you know those games are rigged so it's pretty unlikely that you will actually win anything. Been there. Done that! Winning God's prize is different, in fact, it's exactly the opposite. Your Father wants you to win and will do everything He can to help you. He will train you, show you the timing you need, and the strategy to succeed. He wants you, His precious child, to win that prize! Just take His hand. He will lead you in the way you should go.

In Genesis 17:1-2 (NKJ), God revealed Himself to Abraham: "*When Abram was ninety-nine years old, the Lord appeared to Abram and said to him, "I am Almighty God; walk before Me and be blameless. And I will make My covenant between Me and you, and will multiply you exceedingly.*" Here God revealed Himself as God Almighty—El Shaddai—and told Abraham he would become the father of a nation. God was going to do the impossible for Abraham. He would be to Abraham what His name revealed: The God Who is More than Enough!

In Psalm 68:5, we learn that God is a father to the fatherless and a defender of widows. He can be the Father you've always hoped for and you can confidently ask Him for what you need. God is still El Shaddai. He will be more than enough for you if you trust Him.

Luke 11:11-13 reads: *"Which of you fathers, if your son asks for a fish, will give him a snake instead? Or if he asks for an egg, will give him a scorpion? If you then, though you are evil, know how to give good gifts to your children, how much more will your Father in heaven give the Holy Spirit to those who ask Him!"* Perhaps you've been disappointed so many times in the past that you wonder whether you can trust anyone ever again. God wants you to know the Holy Spirit inside you will equip and enable you. Trust Him to free you from your past and move you forward into your future. He wants to give you the best.

Have you discovered you really don't like yourself and question how God ever could? Besides, you don't like anyone else either! Before you can like anyone, you need to forgive yourself and other people. God isn't holding anything against you. Tell God you are sorry for all the mistakes you have made. God says He will remove your transgressions as far as the east is from the west, remembering your sins no more.

There. Doesn't that feel better? Hey, the tape isn't holding your Glasses together anymore. They look great! Are they new?

Allow God's plan for you to live an abundant life with Him

to come to pass. That doesn't necessarily mean you'll be rich and famous, but it does mean your needs will be met. Your performance level, behavior, church attendance, or Bible study will not cause God to love you any more or any less. Jesus will meet your needs simply because He loves you.

Nothing you have done or will do can make God approve of you. He already does! That may be hard for you to accept. You may have been programmed to think you have to *do* something to gain His approval. Your works won't make Him see you as a better person or get you into heaven. There's no boasting allowed. Your belief in Jesus and what He did for you is your ticket to friendship with the Father for eternity. It's a free gift but it isn't cheap. It cost Jesus everything to get it for you. He did it because you are precious and valuable to Him and His love for you is exceedingly great!

God's perfect 20/20 vision will give you His perfect truth. Let His light flood in and illuminate every step you take in your life from now on. Your newfound ability to see clearly, God's way, will allow you to see His masterpieces everywhere you look. Wear your God Glasses and start hanging out with Jesus, your best friend. He has so much to show you. The more you hang out with Him, the more you will want to hang out with Him! Watch what happens when He gives you His perspective on every aspect of your life. You will be amazed.

Excuse me, but what's that up ahead? Can you see it? It's your future and …*oh*, it's a *bright* one!

QUITTING IS USUALLY A LONG TERM SOLUTION TO A SHORT TERM PROBLEM.

–ANONYMOUS

After Words

receiving and wearing your own God glasses

I hope you have enjoyed learning about God Glasses and how they can change your view of people, circumstances, and life itself. Now that you understand their significance, would you ever want to be limited just to what your natural eyes can see? God's 20/20 perspective will change your life forever. I encourage you to wear your God Glasses every day and to enjoy the extraordinary God-adventure that awaits you as you draw closer to Jesus in friendship and love.

If you don't have God Glasses yet and you would like a pair, all you have to do is ask Jesus into your life, begin reading the Bible to increase your knowledge of Him and enjoy spending time with your new best friend.

God sent Jesus Christ to be the Savior of the world. Romans 10: 9-10 (TLB) says, *"For if you tell others with your own mouth that Jesus Christ is your Lord and believe in your own heart that*

God has raised Him from the dead, you will be saved. For it is by believing in his heart that a man becomes right with God; and with his mouth he tells others of his faith, confirming his salvation."

Pray this prayer to begin your friendship with Jesus:

Heavenly Father, I acknowledge that I need Your help. I am not able to change my life or circumstances through my own efforts. I know I have made some wrong decisions. I turn away from my old ways and accept a new life with you. I believe You have provided a way to receive blessings and help; that way is Jesus. Right now, I believe and proclaim Jesus as my Lord and Savior. I ask You to come and give me new life. I want to live for You. Thank You for forgiving me and erasing all of my sins. I receive Your grace and mercy today. Amen.

If this book has impacted your life and you've started wearing your God Glasses, we'd love to hear about your new perspective and adventures with God. Please email us at:

connect@LindaYoungMinistries.com

God Glasses correct our vision—not by
denying the truth—but by revealing it.

Author

Linda Young is a passionate author and teacher who delights in seeing lives transformed with the message of God's goodness and unconditional love. Having experienced God's grace and forgiveness in their own lives and drawing from that freedom, Linda and her husband, Ray, founded Linda Young Ministries.

Individuals, small groups, and large audiences are drawn to her unassuming approachable humanness where mistakes happen, but so does love. Linda is the neighbor you can have coffee with, a friend sitting across from you on the sofa. Her unique television program, **LINDA YOUNG** Ⓛ **KNOWING GOD**, airs weekly on the Total Living Network (TLN) in select cities and on Sky Angel nationwide.

Linda is a conference speaker and women's retreat leader known for her vibrant yet down-to-earth teaching style, packed with encouragement and delivered from a place of genuine love for people.

Linda holds an MAR with an emphasis in Christian Leadership from Liberty Theological Seminary and is a member of the pastoral staff at Church 212° in La Quinta, California. She and her husband, Ray, make their home in Rancho Mirage, California. They have six grown children and three grandchildren.

Contact

To order additional copies of this book and other products
by Linda Young please visit our online store at:

LindaYoungMinistries.com

GOD GLASSES
is published by Ray and Linda Young
Palm Desert, CA